WHAT'S IN *Wodehouse*

CHARLES E. GOULD, JR., *teaches English at Kent School, Connecticut and repairs reed organs in Kennebunkport, Maine. Any time he has to spare, he spends usefully wallowing in Wodehouse.*

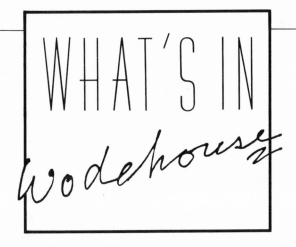

WHAT'S IN Wodehouse

OR
JEEVES HAS GONE A-SHRIMPING AND
THE FAT PIG HAS GROWN
EVEN STOUTER

CHARLES E. GOULD, JR.

H
JAMES H. HEINEMAN, INC., NEW YORK.

Line illustrations, numbers 1 through 12 inclusive, by Peter van Straaten

First published in the United States in 1989
by James H. Heineman, Inc.,

FOR CAROLYN

CONTENTS

ACKNOWLEDGMENTS

Apart from the Giants of the Industry on whom I have relied in the production of this slender volume, whom I have trusted without fail—Daniel H. Garrison, James H. Heineman, Geoffrey Jaggard, David A. Jasen, Eileen McIlvaine, Norman Murphy and Richard Usborne—I am much indebted besides to the patient Griseldas, Poorhouse Maggies willing to bear the yoke, and Young Lochinvars come out of the West who enabled me to get this thing out of my head, if not out of my system: O.B. Davis, Senior Master at Kent School; Judith Dike, Librarian at Kent School; Claude Saucy, Chairman of Art at Kent School; and Diana Yammin, my colleague at Kent School who proofread the pages as I typed them, checked and chuckled over the puzzles, found them good even though knowing no Wodehouse, and did her job and most of mine at the same time. My particular thanks are due to Jimmy Heineman, who had the idea and gave it to me; to Richard Usborne, the bright ray who kindled all this fire; and to Emily Elliot Gould, who smiles upon rather than at my labors.

I could have written *Spindrift* alone. Almost anybody could. But the Present Volume, as they call it, is really the work of three: P.G. Wodehouse, Jimmy Heineman, and the Rest of Us.

FOREWORD

DANIEL H. GARRISON

Leisurely reader: having disposed of the pleas of your friends and relatives and the adjurations of moralists that life is real and life is earnest and life is more than rereading the seventy-odd novels and 300-odd stories of Pelham Grenville Wodehouse (and some of them *are* pretty odd), you are now ready to enter the lists of the Muses and joust with the experts on the finer points of Wodehousiana.

The matter alluded to in these pages is nothing less than the *arcana suprema* of Wodehouse fiction (if you can call it that). The work of the philosopher is to conduct a life of such freedom from distraction as to afford occasional glimpses into these great truths. Far from profaning these arcana by proclaiming them promiscuously to the *profanum vulgus*, the mission of the present volume is to communicate darkly in what way enlightenment lies, and then to reward the pure of heart whose pleasant labors have led them to epiphany.

Enlightenment and recognition were not always so easily achieved: the selfless labors of saintly drudges, sparkling sages, and pious publishers have now enabled the humblest hewer of wood and drawer of water to build a cheap but impressive library of Wodehouse fiction, Wodehouse handbooks and vademecums, and Wodehouse guides to the perplexed. Brave woodmen go daily into dark forests to cut stout lumber for bookcases, while fearless miners toil deep beneath the earth for coal to light the lamps of learning far into the night.

Yet there is no royal road to higher knowledge. The answers to the great mysteries hinted herein lie deep within the *ipsissima verba* of the Master himself, not in the glib formulations of his acolytes.

Reader, perpend: *forsan et haec olim meminisse iuvabit!*

DANIEL H. GARRISON, PhD
Hellenist, Latinist
Professor, Northwestern University

PREFACE

A LETTER TO THE PUBLISHER

Dear Jimmy:

Rather than write the customary Introduction I am following the example of Stella Gibbons in *Cold Comfort Farm,* a novel which—apart from *Right Ho Jeeves* and *Hot Water*—ranks with *Lucky Jim* in my estimation as one of the funniest ever written in English, where she addresses in epistolary style a friend and mentor much as I now address you. Thank you, first of all, for conceiving, proposing, inspiring and enduring what I imagine reviewers will in large numbers soon be referring to as "the present volume." Having said that, I may now turn to the concerns of our reading public.

"Why a quiz?" they may well be asking themselves. I find that a tough one to answer. In the minds of my students, quizzes are the work of churls and dastards; but grown-ups seem to like them. The Texaco Opera Quiz has been popular for decades. People have been putting up with Socrates' incessant pestering of Glaucon for centuries. There are endless Sherlock Holmes quizzes, and the Baker Street Irregulars are not to be outdone by the Janeites, who have counted every tumbler drawn of the waters in the Pump Room at Bath, every locked chest and secret passage at Northanger Abbey, and every common cold in the

comparatively few works by Miss Austen—to whom the word
quiz, incidentally, meant not what it means to us but rather *an
odd-looking thing.* (Our use of the word to mean *questions on major
or minor details* is American slang, only a few years older than
Wodehouse himself, according to the OED.) There have been
Wodehouse quizzes; but your idea that there should be an
Empress among them has interested me strangely. Besides being
fun for all those present, it has seemed to me to offer potential
for a sort of canonization, never before attempted in this way, of
certain important features of Wodehouse's art. Daniel Garrison,
Geoffrey Jaggard, David Jasen and Richard Usborne have in vast
and various ways canonized much of Wodehousean writ; but, in
a manner of speaking, all they've come up with is answers. Here,
I make bold to give you the questions! (Some of which,
incidentally, cannot be solved by looking into their Indices). In
so doing I have tried to arrange things for both instruction and
delight. One question followed by another question followed by
another question until we got to 1001 could turn pretty boring
by the time we got to number 10, and then all the weary work to
do over again a hundred times. But the format which follows
attempts if not Cleopatra's infinite variety at least enough variety
that time cannot stale nor custom wither it. Part of my devilish
cunning has been to make some of the questions more puzzles
than questions, and part has been to make some of the
questions supply answers to others. The organizing principle, as
you will soon discover, is of the It's-a-poor-thing-but-mine-own
class: it makes perfect, unassailable sense to me, one man's
thingummy being another man's major general. And finally, I am
adapting another device of Stella Gibbons, which she attributes
to "the late Herr Baedeker," marking what I consider to be the
finer or more difficult questions with one [*], two [* *] or three
[* * *] asterisks. "In such a manner," she writes, "did the good
man deal with cathedrals, hotels and paintings by men of genius.
There seems no reason why it should not be applied to passages
in novels." Or to questions in quizzes. To you and your readers,

then, I now offer this odd-looking thing, this Fat Pig of a Quiz.
Go to it—and may heaven speed not only your Whoing, but also
your Whatting, Whereing and Whenning.

Yours ever,

CHARLES E. GOULD, JR.

Kennebunkport
December 1989

A LETTER FROM
THE PUBLISHER

AND

THE SUMMA CUM LAUDE

DIPLOMA

The notion for this book originated several years ago, when the idea of 101—or perhaps even 1001—questions about the Works of Wodehouse came to me one evening as a way to cultivate interest in The Master. It has become clear in the time since that such interest needs no cultivating: like Topsy, it grows daily; but the idea in its present shape is still less a harvest than a planting. Many of the puzzles and questions will be, for the average Wodehousean, the work of a moment to solve or answer; others will be a challenge to the most learned. The author himself professes inability to handle some of them at a glance, allowing further that many of his answers are incomplete, some perhaps inaccurate, and all of them utterly bewildering to the student of Dostoyevsky. Those that yet remain in his mind are even more perplexing.

Be that as it may, the Publisher wishes to honor those serious students of Wodehouse who approach this volume in the proper spirit of solemnity—like, as it were, Beach beating the Dinner Gong, Chester Meredith planning an approach shot, or Jeeves eyeing the young master's white tie. To that end, we offer the Wodehouse Summa Cum Laude Diploma to all those (whether their voices have broken before the second Sunday in Epiphany or not) who turn in a complete set of responses to the questions in Chapter XXIV, "Le Dernier Cri," which is designed as a comprehensive albeit sketchy test of your Wodehouse knowledge and ingenuity. Please send your responses, numbered in order on a single sheet, to the address below—including, of course, the name to appear on your Diploma and the address to which it should be sent.

JIMMY HEINEMAN

PETER HERBERT

c/o JAMES H. HEINEMAN, INC., PUBLISHERS,
475 PARK AVENUE,
NEW YORK, NY 10022

WHAT'S IN

Wodehouse

PLUMMING THE
DEPTHS

E specially when in the grip of the Bertie and Blandings sagas, but also when bitten by the school, golf, Mulliner, Hollywood and Psmith bugs, Wodehouse created not one but several literary worlds, each of which has its own population, map and distinctive style. Sometimes, of course, they overlap. The questions in this chapter are concerned with essential images and events of those various worlds.

1. What is Jeeves's first name?

2. What is Bertie's middle name?

3. Who is the Sebastian Bach of Butlers?

4. What two people, what two pigs, compete annually in Shropshire?

5. Who wouldn't have done for the Duke? [* * *]

6. Who favored Nietzsche, who thought him fundamentally unsound, and who didn't know who he was?

7. What great writer thought P.G. Wodehouse "not bad?" [* *]

8. When Cuthbert Dibble, Orlo Hough, James Bates, Francis Heppenstall, Leonard Starkie and five others also ran, who won?

9. Who appeared in "Madame's Nightshirt," wearing what?

10. Whose sister appeared in the movies?

11. Where are the upper slopes upon which ice formed?

12. Club on Curzon Street?

13. Hotel on Clarges Street?

14. What is a pothunter?

15. What is a gold bat?

16. What is a white feather?

17. What writer, where, called Wodehouse the best living writer of English, "the head of my profession"?

18. What writer called Wodehouse "the performing flea of English literature"? What did Wodehouse do in return?

19. What is the Jeeves novel in which Bertie does not appear?

20. What is the Jeeves story in which Bertie is not the narrator?

21. What is the title of the novel whose title is the title of a novel within the novel?

22. Where is it suggested (only once) that Bertie wears a monocle? [* * *]

23. What American writer described Bolton, Wodehouse and Kern as her "favorite indoor sport"?

24. What writer is the published authority on the diet of pigs, affirming that the proper caloric intake is 57,800 per day?

25. Bertie's "good and deserving" aunt?

26. Bertie's aunt who "wears barbed wire next the skin?"

27. Bertie's third aunt—not so well-known? [* * *]

28. Lord Emsworth's deceased brother? [* * *]

THAT WAS NO LADY, THAT WAS . . .

Clarence, Ninth Earl of Emsworth, has ten sisters. Who are they?

29. Lord Emsworth's sister (1)

30. Lord Emsworth's sister (2)

31. Lord Emsworth's sister (3)

32. Lord Emsworth's sister (4)

33. Lord Emsworth's sister (5)

34. Lord Emsworth's sister (6)

35. Lord Emsworth's sister (7)

36. Lord Emsworth's sister (8)

37. Lord Emsworth's sister (9)

38. Lord Emsworth's sister (10)

* * *

39. Who is Bertie Wooster's (only) sister?

40. What is the most significant fact about *Not Now, Jeeves!*?

41. Bertie's twin cousins were sent down. Why?

42. Who was the simultaneous girl they loved?

43. You're in London. You want, like everyone else, to be at Blandings Castle. You are 5'11" in your dancing shoes, you are a clean-shaven male, you weigh exactly the same as your I.Q. At which London Terminus do you board the train for Blandings Castle?

44. All of the foregoing truths obtaining, where do you get off?

45. If you want to go to Paris by train, at which London Terminus do you avoid meeting Lady Julia Fish?

46. What, specifically, brought Bertram Wooster to America for the first time? (Motive, not conveyance.)

47. When did P.G. Wodehouse come to America for the first time?

IN VINO VERITAS

Bertie Wooster identifies six distinct varieties of hangover. What are they?

48. Hangover #1

49. Hangover #2

50. Hangover #3

51. Hangover #4

52. Hangover #5

53. Hangover #6

54. Who mistook a coal scuttle for a mad dog and tried to shoot it with the fire tongs? Says who? Where?   [*]

55. What sober judge attributes his shadow to drink?

56. To what Wodehouse character is the phenomenon of a hangover apparently unknown, despite his regarding alcohol as a sort of food (as an Uncle of Bertie's was the first to discover it is)?

57. Who is the Uncle who made that useful discovery?

58. And what penance, from time to time, must he pay?

*   *   *

59. J. Sheringham Adair offers as his best agents Meredith and Schwed. Identify Meredith, identify Schwed.

60. What door is guarded by a Ruritanian Field Marshal?

61. Who spends much of his time at Totleigh Towers under Bertie's bed?

62. Why does he like it there?

63. What is the story, in which collection of stories, in which Jeeves appears for the first time?

64. In that story, he speaks only twice. What does he say?

65. In that same story, Bertie is not known by the surname for which he is now famous. What *is* his surname in that story?

66. Who is Reggie Pepper? Why is he important?

A SEIZURE OF AUNTS

Jeeves has twice as many aunts as Bertie Wooster, for a grand total of six.
Surprised? Identify each by name or distinguishing trait.

67. Jeeves's Aunt (1)

68. Jeeves's Aunt (2)

69. Jeeves's Aunt (3)

70. Jeeves's Aunt (4)

71. Jeeves's Aunt (5)

72. Jeeves's Aunt (6)

* * *

73. Who is the dumbest blonde in Shropshire, if not in all the world?

74. Bertie went to school in Bramley-on-Sea. Name the school.

75. Name its Headmaster.

76. In what story does PGW slip up about the name of the school, giving it the same Headmaster and location but a different name?

77. In what novel does Wodehouse get the school right but makes a bloomer about the name of the Headmaster?

78. Bertie won two prizes there: what are they?

79. After Malvern House, what academic groves did Wooster haunt?

80. Whose laugh is a noise like the Scotch express going under a bridge?

81. Who regards the stars as God's Daisy-Chain?

82. Who won a Scripture Prize by taking a list of the Kings of Judah into the examination room, tucked into her middy blouse? [* *]

83. Whom does Augustus Fink-Nottle accuse of similar malfeasance? [* *]

84. Valley Fields is drawn from what London suburb?

85. What is the significance of that suburb to Wodehouse's own life?

86. Name two movie studios from Wodehouse fiction.

87. Name two movies based on Wodehouse books, with the same title as the book.

88. In general, there are two distinctly different settings for the Wodehouse golf stories. What are they?

89. Who presides over, and narrates the stories of, each?

90. What actor first portrayed Jeeves on the screen?

91. What actor portrayed Lord Emsworth for B.B.C. Television?

92. What actor portrayed Jeeves for B.B.C. Television?

93. What actor has portrayed Bertie in England, Canada and America?

94. What is the school of most of the School Stories?

95. Who are the Charter Members of Bachelors Anonymous?

96. Name a couple of crooks in Wodehouse—better yet, name *two* couples, both married.

97. Who is Leonora?

98. What is Wodehouse's Degree?

99. What is Wodehouse's Title?

100. There is a Lorimer in a Wodehouse story, and a more important Lorimer in the story of Wodehouse's life. Identify each. [* *]

ANSWERS

CHAPTER I · PLUMMING THE DEPTHS

1. *Reginald.*

2. *Wilberforce.*

3. *Sebastian Beach.*

4. *Lord Emsworth, The Empress of Blandings* vs. *Sir Gregory Parsloe-Parsloe, The Pride of Matchingham.*

5. *Bradbury Fisher's mother-in-law. ("Keeping In with Vosper")*

6. *Florence Craye, Jeeves, Bertie Wooster. ("Jeeves Takes Charge")*

7. *Vladimir Brusiloff. ("The Clicking of Cuthbert")*

8. *James Bates. ("The Great Sermon Handicap")*

9. *Bertram Wooster, wearing What the Well-Dressed Man is Wearing ("Clustering Round Young Bingo,"* Jeeves and the Feudal Spirit, *Ch. 11,* passim.)

10. *Catsmeat Potter-Pirbright's sister Corky, as Cora Starr.* (The Mating Season)

11. *Beach's forehead.*

12. *The Junior Ganymede, Jeeve's club.* (The Code of the Woosters, passim.)

13. *Barribault's, in* Ice in the Bedroom, *elsewhere* (passim) *placed in Brook Street where Claridge's, presumably its model, actually is.*

14. *A schoolboy in quest of missing trophies.*

15. *A miniature cricket bat.*

16. *A symbol of cowardice.*

17. *Hilaire Belloc, in the Preface to* Week-End Wodehouse.

18. *Sean O'Casey. Wodehouse took the phrase as the title of a semiautobiographical book.*

19. Ring for Jeeves/The Return of Jeeves.

20. *"Bertie Changes His Mind."*

21. Cocktail Time.

22. *"The Spot of Art"*

23. *Dorothy Parker.*

24. *Wolff-Lehmann.* (Service with a Smile, A Pelican at Blandings)

25. *Aunt Dahlia.*

26. *Aunt Agatha.*

27. *Aunt Emily, mother of Claude and Eustace ("The Delayed Exit of Claude and Eustace," an Aunt by marriage.)*

28. *The late Hon. Lancelot Threepwood.* (Summer Lightning)

29. *Lady Ann Warblington.* (Something Fresh)

30. *Lady Charlotte. ("The Crime Wave at Blandings")*

31. *Lady Constance Keeble, later Schoonmaker.* (Passim)

32. *Georgiana, Lady Alcester, Marchioness of Alcester.* (Blandings Castle).

33. *Lady Hermione Wedge.* (Passim)

34. *Lady Dora Garland.* (Full Moon, Pigs Have Wings)

35. *Lady Julia Fish.* (Heavy Weather, Summer Lighting/Fish Preferred)

36. *Lady Jane Allsop (?), mother of Angela ("Pig-Hoo-o-o-o-ey!") and perhaps of Wilfred Allsop (Galahad at Blandings).*

37. *Lady Florence.* (Sunset at Blandings)

38. *Lady Diana.* (Sunset at Blandings)

39. *Mrs. Scholfield. ("Bertie Changes His Mind")*

40. *Not written. No such thing.*

41. *They poured lemonade on the Junior Dean of their college. "I see nothing amusing in the outrage."*
    "Sent down" means dismissed or suspended from the University as a punishment. *("The Delayed Exit of Claude and Eustace")*

42. *Marion Wardour. ("The Delayed Exit of Claude and Eustace")*

43. *Paddington.*

44. *Market Blandings.*

45. *Victoria, or Charing Cross.*

46. *Bertie (as Bertie Mannering-Phipps) is first sent to New York by Aunt Agatha Gregson to extricate his cousin Gussie from his entanglement with Ray Denison, a vaudeville singer ("Extricating Young Gussie"). Failing in this assignment, he finds it "a sound scheme to stop on" ("The Artistic Career of Corky"), and occasionally thereafter (when France seems too close) to return.*

47. *1904, arriving on April 25.*

48. *The Atomic* —The Mating Season, *Chapter 3*

49. *The Broken Compass* —Ibid.

50. *The Cement Mixer* —Ibid.

51. *The Comet* —Ibid.

52. *The Gremlin Bogie* —Ibid.

53. *The Sewing Machine* —Ibid.

54. *Colonel Miles (formerly "Fishy") Fish, in the early morning of New Year's Day, 1902. Galahad Threepwood dismays his sister Lady Julia with this account in Chapter X of* Heavy Weather.

55. *Tipton Plimsoll.* (Full Moon)

56. *Galahad Threepwood. (Passim)*

57. *Uncle George, Lord Yaxley. ("The Delayed Exit of Claude and Eustace")*

58. *He goes to Harrogate or Carlsbad to Take the Cure. ("Indian Summer of an Uncle," passim)*

59. *Meredith: Wodehouse's New York Literary Agent, Scott Meredith. Schwed: Peter Schwed, Wodehouse's Editor and Publisher at Simon & Schuster, a friend and aficionado.*

60. *The front door of Barribault's Hotel.* (Something Fishy, Full Moon)

61. *Gussie Fink-Nottle.* (The Code of the Woosters)

62. *It is a Spode-Free Environment.* (The Code of the Woosters)

63. *"Extricating Young Gussie," in* The Man with Two Left Feet.

64. *"Mrs. Gregson to see you, sir," and "Very good, sir; which suit will you wear," in "Extricating Young Gussie."*

65. *Bertie Mannering-Phipps.*

66. *He is the latent literary forebear of Bertie Wooster, a rich uncle's heir, narrator of his own stories. Jeeves does not appear in them, but "Helping Freddie" ("Lines and Business") in* My Man Jeeves *and "Doing Clarence A Bit of Good" in* The Man With Two Left Feet *foreshadow later revision into Jeeves stories: "Fixing it for Freddie"* (Carry On, Jeeves) *and "Jeeves Makes an Omelette"* (A Few Quick Ones).

67. *The martyr to swollen limbs until cured by Walksinshaw's Supreme Ointment. ("Jeeves Takes Charge")*

68. *The Rosie M. Banks fan. ("Jeeves Exerts the Old Cerebellum")*

69. *The impassioned taxicab rider. ("The Aunt and the Sluggard")*

70. *Aunt Annie, disliked by all members of the family.* (Right Ho, Jeeves)

71. *Aunt Emily, interested in psychic research.* (Ring for Jeeves)

72. *Mrs. P.B. Pigott, Balmoral, Mafeking Road, Maiden Eggesford, Somerset (Aunts Aren't Gentlemen). Of course, since three of these aunts aren't named, there is no proving that there are more than the three, doubling up on their manic imperfections, which are of use to Jeeves in his study of the Psychology of the Individual.*

73. *Veronica Wedge, Lord Emsworth's niece.* (Galahad at Blandings, passim)

74. *Malvern House.* (The Mating Season, *passim*)

75. *Aubrey Upjohn, M.A.*

76. *"Bramley Is So Bracing." (St. Asaph's)*

77. Much Obliged, Jeeves/Jeeves and the Tie that Binds. *(Arnold Abney, M.A.)*

78. *One for Scripture Knowledge, one for Best Collection of Wildflowers. (Passim; "No Wedding Bells for Bingo")*

79. *Eton; Magdalen College, Oxford.* (The Mating Season, Aunts Aren't Gentlemen, passim)

80. *Honoria Glossop's. ("The Pride of the Woosters is Wounded")*

81. *Madeline Bassett.* (The Mating Season, passim)

82. *Mrs. Bingo Little. ("Jeeves and the Old School Chum")*

83. *B.W. Wooster.* (Right Ho, *Jeeves*)

84. *East Dulwich.*

85. *Dulwich College is there.*

86. *Superba-Llewellyn. Perfecto-Zissbaum.*

87. The Girl on the Boat *(1961)*
    A Damsel in Distress *(1937)*
    Thank You, Jeeves *(1936)*
    Piccadilly Jim *(1936)*
    Summer Lightning *(1933)*
      Silent Films
    The Small Bachelor *(1927)*
    The Clicking of Cuthbert *(1924)*
    A Gentleman of Leisure *(1923)*
    Their Mutual Child *(1920)*
    Damsel in Distress *(1920)*
    The Prince and Betty *(1920)*
    Piccadilly Jim *(1919)*
    Uneasy Money *(1917)*
    Gentleman of Leisure *(1915)*
    (List from Eileen McIlvaine)

88. *England (Woodhaven, Marvis Bay) and Long Island (Manhooset, Goldenville, Squashy Hollow).* (The Clicking of Cuthbert/Golf Without Tears *and* The Heart of a Goof/Divots)

89. *The Oldest Member, on both sides of the Atlantic.*

90. *Arthur Treacher.*

91. *Sir Ralph Richardson.*

92. *Ian Carmichael*

93. *Edward Duke.*

94. *Wrkyn.*

95. *Ephraim Trout, Fred Basset, Johnny Runcible and J.G. Flannery.*

96. *Thos. G. ("Soapy") and Dora ("Dolly") Molloy.* (Sam the Sudden, passim) *Gordon ("Oily") and Gertrude ("Sweetie") Carlisle.* (Hot Water, Cocktail Time)

97. *Wodehouse's step-daughter: only child of Ethel Rowley Wodehouse.*

98. *D.Litt. (Hon.), Oxford, 21 June 1939.*

99. *Sir Pelham*

100. *In* A Perfect's Uncle, *Lorimer shares a study with Pringle in the School-House, Beckford College. He takes the place of Gethryn on the cricket team.*
George Horace Lorimer, Editor-in-Chief of the Saturday Evening Post *from 1899 to 1936, bought* Something New *and* "Extricating Young Gussie," *thus introducing Blandings and Jeeves to the American Periodical public, and beginning an association that lasted fifty years.*

WEDDING BELLES

*A*t the moment I can think of only one divorce in Wodehouse, but there are dozens of marriages, hundreds of engagements. Questions in this chapter are concerned with women involved . . . or not involved.

1. Who is Bertie's cousin by marriage who, thanks to Jeeves's efforts, does not become Bertie's *wife* by marriage?

2. With whom did Jeeves once have an understanding?

3. A Pekingesque who elopes with a Newt fancier? [*]

4. "One of these girls who enjoy in equal quantities the gall of an army mule and the calm insouciance of a fish on a slab of ice" is engaged to whom?

5. "I can't explain; it's surely not his brain that makes me thrill" is a common enough sentiment amongst Wodehouse heroines. What character first put it that way? [* * *]

6. From the Criterion Bar to Matchingham Hall, with the blessing of an Uncle at Blandings?

7. She needed an umbrella, and the Hon. Hugo Walderwick's happened to be in reach.

8. She loved, honored, cherished her shark.

9. Sought by Claude and Eustace—Nights (not Knights) In Arms.

10. From top-knot to shoe sole, The Woman Whom God Forgot."

11. Who counsels against taking up with a Gwladys, a Kathryn, an Ysobel, an Ethyl or a Mabelle?

12. Eponymously named for Laughing Love God's February Festival? [* *]

13. Cousin of Jeeves engaged to an Herefordshire Heir?

14. The divorcée mentioned above, the "sand in civilization's spinach"—who is she?

15. "There is nothing like a dame." Lady Constance hoped Clarence would marry this one.

16. Laid end to end, not that you could do it, they'd reach from Piccadilly Circus to Hyde Park Corner.

17. She is swept off her feet by an imitation of a hen laying an egg.

18. Who is the Amazon Golfer, who eventually writes a novel, engaged intermittently to the same man, in stories written over a span of 37 years?

19. Who marries a man for his hidden lexicon of unprintable words?

20. Who breaks an engagement on account of a dog?

21. Who is the red-head of whom Jeeves, sensibly, does not approve?

22. Who is the red-head who pesters Lord Emsworth?

23. Who is the only female known to appear in pajamas in Bertie's bedroom?

THERE BUT FOR THE GRACE
OF JEEVES GOES BERTRAM

Name 11 Misses, or Near-Misses, whom Bertie Didn't Marry
(*In Alphabetical Order*)

24.

25.

26.

27.

28. [* * *]

29.

30.

31. [* *]

32.

33.

34. [*]

JANE AUSTEN: TAKE A BOW...
AND A BACK SEAT

35. Of Wodehouse's Straight Janes, this one comes close to wrecking the home.

36. A Jane who has her eye on Anatole.

37. The Jane to whom we are told to leave it.

38. The Jane who can dominate Uncle Fred.

39. An eponymous Hockey Captain Jane.

40. A Gem-Stone Jane, secretly engaged to a loser but in love with a winner.

41. A Widgeon-Seven-driving Jane.

42. A Jane who is stuck on a jury.

43. A Plain Jane whose name is Heloise.

44. The Jane who is the third prettiest girl in Shropshire.

45. Augustine Mulliner's Jane.

46. An octogenarian Jane, an ailurophilical Jane.

47. The Jane whose guest is the beautiful Felicia Blakeney.

48. An Old Nanny Jane, living in Valley Fields. (*)

49. The 6th Viscount's Jane, and Bill's too.

50. A Mary Jane, and a cook.

51. A Gourmet Jane who marries a Gourmand.

ANSWERS

CHAPTER II · WEDDING BELLES

1. *Lady Florence Craye, daughter of Percy, Earl of Worplesdon, stepdaughter to Aunt Agatha.* (Joy in the Morning)

2. *In "Jeeves Exerts the Old Cerebellum," first with Miss Watson, Bingo's Uncle Mortimer Little's gourmet cook, then with Mabel, the tea-and-bun shop waitress with whom Bingo Little is infatuated earlier in the same story. There are two extremes here, at least; out of the frying pan, into the sparkling limado about sums it up.*

3. *Emerald Stoker, described in* **Stiff** Upper Lip, Jeeves *as looking like a Pekingese with freckles, elopes with Gussie Fink-Nottle.*

4. *Described thus in* The Code of the Woosters *(Chapter Eight), Stephanie ("Stiffy") Byng is engaged to the Reverend Harold ("Stinker") Pinker.*

5. *Julie LaVerne. ("Bill" in* Showboat*)*

6. *Maudie Stubbs, a former barmaid at the Criterion in London under the name Maudie Montrose, is reunited with Sir Gregory Parsloe in* Pigs Have Wings, *married to him in* Service with a Smile.

7. *Eve Halliday.* (Leave it to Psmith)

8. *Angela Travers, Bertie's cousin.* (Right Ho, Jeeves)

9. *Marion Wardour. ("The Delayed Exit of Claude and Eustace")*

10. *Madeline Basset.* (The Mating Season, passim)

11. *Aunt Dahlia. ("The Spot of Art")*

12. *Joan Valentine.* (Something New)

13. *Mabel, engaged to Charles Edward "Biffy" Biffen who loses her for an absent-minded period during which he becomes engaged to Honoria Glossop, in "The Rummy Affair of Old Biffy."*

14. *Heloise, Princess von und zu Dwornitzchek.* (Summer Moonshine)

15. *Dame Daphne Winkworth.* (Galahad at Blandings)

16. *The girls Freddie Widgeon has loved and lost.* (Young Men in Spats, passim)

17. *Aurelia Cammarleigh. Archibald Mulliner is the* artiste. *("The Reverent Wooing of Archibald")*

18. *Agnes Flack.* (Mr. Mulliner Speaking *through* Plum Pie)

19. *Felicia Blakeney. ("Chester Forgets Himself")*

20. *Agnes Flack. The dog is a Hazard. ("Feet of Clay")*

21. *Roberta Wickham. ("Jeeves and the Yuletide Spirit," passim)*

22. *Sandy Callendar, in her role as Secretary.* (Galahad at Blandings)

23. *Pauline Stoker. The pajamas—heliotrope—are his.* (Thank You, Jeeves)

24. *Madeline Basset.* (Passim)

25. *Vanessa Cook.* (Aunts Aren't Gentlemen)

26. *Florence Craye.* (Passim)

27. *Honoria Glossop.* (Passim)

28. *Miss Mapleton. Not on the boards. ("Jeeves and the Kid Clementina")*

29. *Gwladys Pendlebury. ("Jeeves and the Spot of Art")*

30. *Corky Pirbright.* (The Mating Season)

31. *Muriel Singer makes Bertie want to stroke her hand and say, "There, there, little one!" or words to that effect in "The Artistic Career of Corky," but no business results.*

32. *Pauline Stoker.* (Thank You, Jeeves)

33. *Bobbie Wickham.* (Passim)

34. *Cynthia Wickhammersley. ("The Great Sermon Handicap")*

35. *Jane Packard Bates.* (Heart of a Goof)

36. *Jane Snettisham. ("Jeeves and the Love that Purifies")*

37. *Jane Witherspoon.* (Leave It To Jane: *Bolton / Wodehouse / Kern*)

38. *Jane, Countess of Ickenham.* (Uncle Fred in the Springtime)

39. *Jane Passenger.* (The Luck of the Bodkins)

40. *Jane Opal.* (Hot Water)

41. *(Jane) Imogen Abbot. (Summer Moonshine)*

42. *Jane Hunnicut.* (The Girl in Blue)

43. *Heloise Pringle. ("Without the Option")*

44. *Lord Emsworth's niece Jane, Lady Charlotte's daughter. ("The Crime Wave at Blandings")*

45. *Jane Brandon. ("Mulliner's Buck-U-Uppo")*

46. *Aunt Jane (Pringle?). ("Without the Option")*

47. *Jane Waterfield.* (*"Chester Forgets Himself"*)

48. *Jane Priestly.* (Bachelor's Anonymous)

49. *Jane Benedick.* (Something Fishy)

50. *Mary Jane Piggott.* (Ring for Jeeves)

51. *Jane Watson, Mortimer Little's Cook, marries him in "Jeeves Exerts the Old Cerebellum."*

N O M S   D E   P L U M

W*hen I mentioned once to Jimmy Heineman that I meant to work up something about Wodehouse's titles, he replied, quick as a red-hot ice-pick going through a pound of butter: "But he had only the one."
And actually, though Professor Garrison's list turns up almost five hundred, in a sense that is true: Wodehouse's titles are all, within a few distinct categories, much like one another—in short, only the one or two. This is not surprising, of course, from an author who wrote books one after the other, sometimes the same one after another; he himself remarked, in the Preface to* Summer Lightning: *"With my superior intelligence, I have outgeneralled the man [a critic] this time by putting in all the old Wodehouse characters under the same names."*

Many of the titles of Wodehouse's novels and short stories are clichés or catch-phrases of some species—in large measure what Richard Usborne calls "pulpit-prose and race-course slang"—whether P. G. Wodehouse himself (or Publishers invoking their rights) invented them. In a great many, however, there is a submerged (sometimes barely) joke, pun or allusion. Below offered is a list of clues: to what title of a novel or story does each lead?

1. The Ant and the Grasshopper. Pun. (Fable) [*]

2. Novel by H.G. Wells (1916)

3. William I (1027-1087; Regnabat 1066-)

4. A series of books by Stephen Potter

5. Novel by Ernest Hemingway

6. "Filer a l'anglaise"

7. Painting by Gainsborough (1727-1788)

8. "There is many a poor-house Maggie that is willing to bear the yoke, "And __ _____ ____ _____ __ _____, but __ _____ _____ ____ __ _____." —Kipling, "The Betrothed"

9. Gangster Cant and Marriage Counsellor Cant. Pun.

10. Al Jolson and Solomon

11. American Hymn, John Fawcett (1740-1817)

12. Psalms, XXX.v

13. Nitrous Oxide

14. Stories by Clarence Day (d 1935)

15. "_____ _____ the Ruins," Poem by Robt. Browning (1855)

16. American Baseball Player, N.Y. Yankees Right-Fielder Tommy Henrich's sobriquet, c. 1949-50, bestowed by announcer Mel Allen.

17. "One _____ of _____ makes the whole world kin." —Shakespeare, *Troilus and Cressida.*

18. Binstead and Wells

19. The Walrus and the Carpenter

20. Plum Pudding

21. "There's a divinity that shapes our ends . . . . " *Hamlet,* Act V.

22. "Whither thou goest, I will go." Old Testament.

23. "To take arms against __ _____ ____ _____" *Hamlet,* Act II

24. Sung by Al Jolson

25. Heavy-bodied beer and heavy-bodied one who drinks it in style. Pun.

26. Song by Vincent Youmans (c. 1930). Pun.

27. U.S. Naval Academy Hymn, by William Whiting (1825-1878).

28. Novel by Jerome K. Jerome.

29. Shadrach, Meshach and Abednego

30. Heavyweight champion

31. Not Michelangelo's

32. Novel by Thomas Hardy (1878), stories by Conan Doyle.

33. Theatrical backer (slang) and light American confection. Pun.

34. Novel by Dickens (1865)

35. Story by Edgar Allan Poe (1845)

36. Poem by Henry Wadsworth Longfellow (1807-1882)

37. Play by Arthur Miller (1915-)

38. Story by Rudyard Kipling

39. Nakedly frightful pun on a cliché.

40. Never said "I Cannot tell a lie."

41. Greek hero's weak spot.

42. Novel by George Barr McCutcheon, 1903. Also motion picture.

43. Wall Street jargon: Blue Chip Stock

44. Wall Street jargon: tied up money

45. Rejection slip.

46. Romance cliché.

47. Play by Benn Levy, in which Edward Everett Horton appeared more than 900 times in the title role.

48. Boys will be boys.

49. Detective Story Cliché.

50. Alcoholics _____ .

51. Seaside promotional.

52. Pirate story cliché.

53. Simeon chicanery.

54. Infelicitous paranomasia of a female sort.

55. Felix Infelicitas .... Felix Somnolent. (Catty Pun.)

56. First of Tennyson's Kingly Idylls

57. 19th Century Primers:

58. Actors' cant: words and actions.

59. Every _____ , _____ and _____ . Why them?

60. Edwardian Beak's tough sentence.

61. Dickens wrote one.

62. "_____ _____ _____ _____
"Wherein I'll catch the conscience of the king."
   —Shakespeare, Hamlet

63. Newspaper advert for a New York flat smaller than Bertie's

64. Wodehouse expressed the hope that his would be included in the list of the Hundred Best Books called by this title. [*]

ANSWERS

CHAPTER III · NOMS DE PLUM

1. *"The Aunt and the Sluggard"*

2. Mr. Britling Sees it Through. *Peter Schwed, whose father owned the original oil paintings used to illustrate the book, thence derived* Bertie Wooster Sees It Through.

3. *William the Conqueror:* Bill the Conqueror

4. *Oneupmanship, Gamesmanship, etc.* The Brinkmanship of Galahad Threepwood.

5. A Farewell to Arms. *"Farewell to Legs"*

6. French Leave.

7. *The Blue Boy.* The Girl in Blue.

8. *"A woman is Only a Woman"*
   "A Good Cigar is a Smoke"

9. *Ice: stolen jewelry; frigidity.* Ice in the Bedroom.

10. *Al Jolson sang "Sonny Boy." The Song of Solomon is the Song of Songs. "Jeeves and the Song of Songs"*

11. *"Blest be the tie that binds / Our hearts in Christian Love."* Jeeves and the Tie that Binds. *Peter Schwed's title for "Much Obliged, Jeeves," the 90th-Birthday Celebration novel. "Over the years I have changed Wodehouse's original title (which Barrie & Jenkins blindly uses) to one I think has a better chance of distinguishing one book from another. Such was the case with* Much Obliged, Jeeves *which I changed to* Jeeves and the Tie that Binds. *In making that suggestion I had to justify it so, as I've sometimes done in the past, I wrote that last page or so in our (Simon & Schuster's) edition in my best imitative Wodehouse style and then sent it along to him for approval and for a rewrite in the matchless style of the master himself. He did approve, he did rewrite the page . . . ."*

—Peter Schwed, in a letter to me, January 21, 1974. "Much obliged" is, of course, a catch-phrase, which PGW himself used often in reply to fan letters—at least in his later years. Jeeves says: "There is no time, sir, at which ties do not matter." I don't know whether Mr. Schwed had that in mind.

12. *"Weeping may endure for a night, but joy cometh in the morning."* Joy in the Morning.

13. Laughing Gas.

14. Life with Father. *"Life with Freddie"*

15. *"Love Among the Ruins."* Love Among the Chickens.

16. The Old Reliable.

17. *"One Touch of Nature."*

18. A Pink 'Un and a Pelican. A Pelican at Blandings.

19. *"The time has come, the Walrus said, to talk of many things, / Of shoes and ships and sealing wax, and whether pigs have wings."* — Lewis Carroll

20. Plum Pie.

21. *"Rough Hew Them How We Will."*

22. *The Book of Ruth. "Ruth in Exile."*

23. *"A Sea of Troubles."*

24. *"Sonny Boy"*

25. *"Stylish Stouts."*

26. *"Tee for Two."*

27. *"O hear us when we cry to thee / For those in peril on the sea." "Those in Peril At the Tee."*

28. Three Men on a Boat. Three Men and a Maid/The Girl on the Boat.

29. *"Tried in the Furnace."*

30. *Dempsey, the "White Hope."*

31. *"The Wigmore Venus."*

32. The Return of the Native, *"The Return of Sherlock Holmes."* The Return of Jeeves.

33. Angel Cake.

34. Our Mutual Friend. Their Mutual Child.

35. *"The Purloined Letter."* The Purloined Paperweight.

36. *"Excelsior."*

37. Death of a Salesman. *"Birth of a Salesman."*

38. *"The Man Who Would Be King."* *"The Man Who Disliked Cats / Gave Up Smoking / Married a Hotel."*

39. No Nudes is Good Nudes.

40. Not George Washington.

41. *"The Heel of Achilles."*

42. Brewster's Millions. Biffen's Millions.

43. Fish Preferred.

44. Frozen Assets.

45. *"The Editor Regrets."*

46. A Damsel in Distress.

47. Springtime for Henry. Company for Henry.

48. *"Cats will be Cats."*

49. The Butler Did It.

50. Bachelors Anonymous.

51. *"Bramley Is So Bracing."*

52. *"Buried Treasure."*

53. *"Monkey Business" / "A Cagey Gorilla."*

54. Aunt's Aren't Gentlemen.

55. The Cat-Nappers.

56. *"The Coming of Arthur."* *"The Coming of Gowf / Bill."*

57. *Latin Without Tears, etc.* Golf Without Tears.

58. *"Lines and Business."*

59. *"Tom, Dick and Harry."*

60. *"Without the Option"* [i.e., *of a Fine*].

61. *"Another Christmas Carol."*

62. The Play's the Thing.

63. *"A small bachelor's apartment."* The Small Bachelor.

64. Summer Lightning. *See PGW's Preface to this title.*

PIGS AND PUMPKINS

*W*odehouse plots are thick with things—*physical objects that can be picked up and put down again. Often they are picked up by people to whom they don't belong. Several such objects are listed below. Identify or comment on the significance of each.*

1. a silver cow creamer
2. a sliver of a pig, compared to The Empress
3. an umbrella in Dover Street
4. an umbrella in the Brompton Road
5. a vase
6. flower pots
7. a Cheops IV Dynasty
8. a portrait of Venus
9. a portrait of Bertie
10. a portrait of an uncle's son
11. purple socks
12. a pot of red paint
13. rugger boots and a water spaniel
14. a top hat
15. the manuscript of a memoir

16. a stable cat

17. a picnic basket containing ham sandwiches, tongue sandwiches, a cold chicken, lobster and a bottle of Bollinger

18. The Club Book

19. plus fours from the Cohen Brothers

20. a pair of Old Etonian spats

21. a string of pearls

22. *Strychnine in the Soup*

23. an alpine hat

24. a stray cat

25. a jug of orange juice

26. a plush Mickey Mouse

27. a framed photograph of Bertram

28. a swan

29. a hostage parrot

30. a statue of the Infant Samuel at prayer

31. a black aberdeen terrier

32. *Spindrift*

33. brown walking shoes

34. J.H. Taylor's shirt stud

35. oranges made of yellow yarn

36. a Piccadilly policeman's helmet

37. Totleigh-in-the Wold constable's helmet

38. a small, leather-covered notebook

39. a steak and kidney pie

40. a kennel of Pekes

41. a flower pot attached to a piece of string

42. a portrait of an ancestor

43. a banjolele

44. an airgun

45. a white mess jacket

46. the Broadway Special

47. soft silk evening shirts

48. mauve shirts

49. three cats and a fish

50. the Love-r-ly Silver Cup

51. a Gutenberg Bible

52. an eye patch

53. a finger-stall

54. pince-nez affixed to ginger-beer wire

55. pince-nez on a string

56. steel-rimmed spectacles

57. a gleaming monocle

58. a black-rimmed monocle

59. an ancient push bike

60. a black beard of Imperial cut

61. a Mephistopheles fancy-dress costume

62. a silver watch

63. a golf ball in Berkeley Mansions

64. a pink chrysanthemum

65. white violets

66. biscuits in a tin

67. a hot-water bottle

68. a volume of Spinoza

69. a tongue, a loaf of bread, a knife, a fork, salt, a corkscrew and a bottle of white wine

70. Marie Lloyd's autograph

71. an elevenpence-ha'penny squirt [* *]

72. The Luminous Rabbit

73. a brass paper fastener

74. a legendary sponge

75. a dead dog [* *]

ANSWERS

CHAPTER IV · PIGS AND PUMPKINS

1. *Sir Watkyn Bassett gets there first.* (Code of the Woosters, passim)

2. *Sir Gregory's Pride of Matchingham gets taken for a ride.* (Pigs Have Wings)

3. *Psmith gives The Hon. Hugo Walderwick's to Eve Halliday, whose need is greater than his.* (Leave it to Psmith)

4. *It's Pop Bassett's, but a primeval instinct makes Bertie reach out for it "like a flower groping toward the sun," in that antique shop where began all the fuss about the cow creamer.* (Code of the Woosters)

5. *"Not in harmony with the appointments of the room," Jeeves says. "And in my excitement, sir, I am sorry to say I broke it beyond repair." ("The Inferiority Complex of Old Sippy")*

6. *Baxter is never able to live down throwing Lord Emsworth's.* (Leave it to Psmith)

7. *Lord Emsworth absent-mindedly pockets the one belonging to J. Preston Peters.* (Something Fresh)

8. *There are three: The Wigmore Venus, painted by Alice Wigmore* (Indiscretions of Archie), *the unbearable Yeardsley Venus ("Doing Clarence a Bit of Good") and the Fothergill Venus ("Jeeves Makes an Omelette"). Oddly, the painters of the latter two want to keep them.*

9. *Gwladys Pendlebury painted it. Jeeves doesn't like it, and points out to Mr. Slingsby of Slingsby's Superb Soups its possibilities as an advertising medium: "There I sat absolutely slavering through a monocle about six inches in circumference at a plateful of soup, looking as if I hadn't had a meal for weeks."* Circumference? *Must mean* diameter. *("Jeeves and the Spot of Art")*

10. *The sitter is the human poached egg who bounces Bruce ("Corky") Corcoran out of his inheritance from Uncle Alexander Worple. The portrait, at Jeeves's suggestion, becomes the foundation for The Adventures of Baby Blobbs.*

11. *Resulting in the startling dressiness of a lift attendant. ("Jeeves and the Chump Cyril")*

12. *Lord Emsworth leaves it carelessly lying about in the museum.* (Something Fresh)

13. *Urgently required for the wooing of Miss Dalgleish. ("Tuppy Changes His Mind")*

14. *Sir Roderick Glossop's is sought by The Seekers ("Sir Roderick Comes to Lunch"), Lord Hoddeston's is replaced by a cap with purple checks* (Big Money), *Psmith's sustains a bullet hole* (Psmith Journalist), *Lord Blicester's is struck squarely abaft the binnacle by a well-aimed Brazil nut ("The Masked Troubadour"). Numerous others* passim.

15. *Lady Constance found it unpalatable, but it fed Gally's appetite for telling the tale: hearty fare, ultimately digested by the Empress of Blandings* (Heavy Weather). *Bertie's Uncle Willoughby's Recollections, on the other hand, Jeeves posts to the publisher (*"Jeeves Takes Charge"*).*

16. *Potato Chip is lost without it: "What asses horses are, Jeeves."* (Aunts Aren't Gentlemen)

17. *Jeeves leaves it behind. (*"Jeeves and the Old School Chum"*)*

18. *Contains the scoop on Eulalie Soeurs* (Code of the Woosters et al.) *It falls into the Wrong Hands in* Much Obliged, Jeeves, *when Rupert Bingley uses it to blackmail Ginger Winship.*

19. *They do wonders for Wallace Chesney's golf, not so much for his appearance. They're finally hot stuff. (*"The Magic Plus Fours"*)*

20. *Jeeves burns them, before breakfast. (*"The Delayed Exit of Claude and Eustace"*)*

21. *Lady Julia Blunt's prove to be paste* (The Intrusion of Jimmy), *Aunt Agatha's prove to be just where she left them (*"Aunt Agatha Takes the Count"*). Others* passim.

22. *Cyril Mulliner leaves his copy on the train, but swipes Lady Bassett's in the dead of night, when Lester Mapledurham (pronounced Mum) swipes it from him. Possession, in this case, is nine points of the In-Law. (*"Strychnine in the Soup"*)*

23. *As worn by Alpine Joe, Wanted by the Police. But the hat itself is unwanted by Jeeves.* (Stiff Upper Lip, Jeeves)

24. *Puts Billy Windsor, and by extension Psmith, in good with Bat Jarvis: "Obliged. Fond of de kit, I am."* (Psmith Journalist)

25. *The old familiar juice added to it in liberal measure, it sloshes against Gussie Fink-Nottle's back teeth as he awards the Prizes at Market Snodsbury Grammar School.* (Right Ho, Jeeves)

26. *A pledge of love from Monty Bodkin to Gertrude Butterwick fancied also by Lottie Blossom for itself alone, and by necklace smugglers for its hollowness.* (The Luck of the Bodkins)

27. *"The drawing room was on the first floor, and the photograph was on the table by the fireplace. Only, if you understand me, it wasn't." (*"Clustering Round Young Bingo"*)*

28. *"As swans go, he may have been well up in the ranks of the intelligentsia; but, when it came to pitting his brains against Jeeves, he was simply wasting his time." The Right Hon. A.B. Filmer can but agree. ("Jeeves and the Impending Doom")*

29. *Stanley Featherstonehaugh Ukridge and Millie kidnap Lady Lakenheath's parrot Leonard. " 'She was terribly worried,' argued the girl. " 'Best thing in the world,' I assured her. 'Too much peace of mind leads to premature old age.' " ("Ukridge Rounds a Nasty Corner")*

30. *"He swept his arm round dramatically, overturning a plaster cast of the Infant Samuel at Prayer. ("Ukridge's Dog College")*
    Dashed to the floor by Aunt Dahlia at Totleigh Towers in The Code of the Woosters. *Elsewhere passim.*

31. *The foul Blumenfeld child takes a fancy to Aunt Agatha's McIntosh ("Jeeves and the Dog McIntosh"). Bartholomew is Stiffy Byng's* (The Code of the Woosters, Stiff Upper Lip, Jeeves).

32. *Just before* Spinoza *on the bookseller's shelf, otherwise a far cry by Florence Craye.* (Joy in the Morning)

33. *"I felt that I should tell you, sir, that somebody has been putting black polish on your brown walking shoes." It was young blighted Edwin, the Boy Scout. ("Jeeves Takes Charge")*

34. *Bradbury Fisher buys it for his collection—only after his wife Evangeline's impulsive engaging of Vosper puts her at his mercy. ("High Stakes")*

35. *The blighter Steggles substitutes the real thing for the Finale—and the Finish—of "What Ho, Twing!!" ("The Metropolitan Touch")*

36. *"But there's a policeman inside it. You can see him distinctly." ("Without the Option")* (Passim.)

37. *Stiffy demands it.* (The Code of the Woosters)

38. *Gussie's, full of good stuff. Prod Stiffy's legs? Egad!* (The Code of the Woosters)

39. *"Do you know, I found him in the larder at one o'clock this morning, absolutely wallowing in a steak and kidney pie."* (Right Ho, Jeeves)

40. *"The place was a sea of Pekingese dogs. Later investigation reduced their number to six, but in that first moment there seemed to be hundreds."* Ukridge intends to make thousands. The dogs, of course, belong to Aunt Julia. *("Ukridge's Dog College")*

41. *How to crash St. Monica's, the school run by Miss Mapleton.* *("Jeeves and the Kid Clementina")*

42. *"The sixth and final shot hit a life-size picture of his lordship's maternal grandmother in the face and improved it out of all knowledge."* (Something Fresh)

43. *"Complaints, it would seem, have been lodged by the Honourable Mrs. Tinkler-Moulke, of C.6; by Lieutenant-Colonel J.J. Bustard, D.S.O., of B.5; and Sir Everard and Lady Blenner-Hassett, of B.7."* And also by Jeeves: *"And let me tell you that better men than you have stood worse than banjoleles. Are you aware that a certain Bulgarian, Elia Gospodinoff, once played the bagpipes for twenty-four hours without a stop?"* (Thank You, Jeeves)

44. *Charlotte Mulliner uses young Wilfred Bassinger's to fire on Colonel Sir Francis Pashley-Drake ("Unpleasantness at Bludleigh Court"). When Lady Constance shoots Beach, the Crime Wave at Blandings finally ebbs.*

45. *"You look like one of the chorus of male guests at Abernethy Towers in Act 2 of a touring musical comedy."* Jeeves, inadvertently of course, leaves a hot iron upon it. (Right-Ho, Jeeves)

46. *"The nub of the thing was that he wanted me to wear the White House Wonder—as worn by President Coolidge—when I had my heart set on the Broadway Special, much patronised by the Younger Set."* It's a hat. *("Jeeves and the Unbidden Guest")*

47. *"Soft silk shirts with evening costume are not worn, sir,"* despite the claim made by Bertie's piece in **Milady's Boudoir**. *("Clustering Round Young Bingo")*

48. *Jeeves sent them back. ("Jeeves Exerts the Old Cerebellum")*

49. *On The Seekers' List, ahead of Truth and Knowledge. Also in Bertie's bedroom. ("Sir Roderick Comes to Lunch")*

50. *Mrs. Charlie, against all the odds, wins it at Geisenheimer's. (The Man with Two Left Feet)*

51. *There's one in the museum at Blandings, side by side with a bullet from the field of Waterloo, one of a consignment of ten thousand shipped there for the use of tourists by a Birmingham firm.* (Something Fresh)

52. *Bill Belfry, d.b.a. Honest Patch Perkins, features one.* (Ring for Jeeves)

53. *Galahad tells the story, in* Pigs Have Wings, *of the time Clarence loses his finger-stall in a salad he is mixing.*

54. *Ukridge's.* Passim.

55. *Lord Emsworth's are elusive.* Passim.

56. *Baxter's give him that steely-eyed look.* Passim.

57. *Psmith's.* Passim.

58. *The Hon. Galahad Threepwood's.* Passim.

59. *"The nuts firm, the brakes in order, the sprockets running true with the differential gear?"*
"Yes, sir." (Right Ho, Jeeves)

60. *"If, say, you were Hawes and Dawes, Shirts, Ties and Linens, twenty-three pounds, four and six, would you imagine for an instant that beneath this shrubbery, Godfrey, Lord Biskerton, lay hid?"*
"Of course I should." (Big Money)

61. *"And scarcely had I opened the door when I heard voices in the sitting-room, and scarcely had I entered the sitting-room when I found that these proceeded from Jeeves and what appeared at first sight to be the Devil.*
"A closer scrutiny informed me that it was Gussie Fink-Nottle, dressed as Mephistopheles." (Right Ho, Jeeves)

62. *Beach's Darts Tournament Trophy, absent-mindedly absconded with by Sam Bagshott.* (Galahad at Blandings)

63. *"Then, once more observing 'Coo!' (or 'Goo!'), he sprang forward, trod on the golf-ball I had been practising putting with, and took one of the finest tosses I have ever witnessed."* ("The Spot of Art")

64. *Freddie Threepwood had a carnation in mind; "Psmith regarded the repellent object with disfavour through his eyeglass."* (Leave it to Psmith)

65. *William Bates sent them, but Jane assumed they were from the blighter Spelvin. ("Jane Gets Off the Fairway")*

66. *The high point of Bertie's formative years, when Aubrey Upjohn, M.A., found him sneaking biscuits from the tin in his study at dead of night.* (The Code of the Woosters, passim.)

67. *With a darning-needle attached to the end of a stick, you can, if you are under the influence of Bobbie Wickham, poke a hole in one. ("Jeeves and the Yuletide Spirit")*

68. *" 'Spinoza, eh? Is he the Book Society's Choice of the Month?'
" 'I believe not, sir.'
" 'Well, he's the only fellow I ever heard of who wasn't.' "*
(Joy in the Morning)

69. *George Emerson purchases them and sets out to convey them to Aline Peters's doormat, but Baxter intervenes—sorely to his regret:
" 'Stuffin' of 'isself at all hours!' said the voice. "* (Something Fresh)

70. *"At the age of fourteen I once wrote to Marie Lloyd for her autograph, but apart from that my private life could bear the strictest investigation." ("The Love that Purifies")*

71. *"Take this, Biffy, with an old friend's blessing, refill the bulb, shove it into Sir Roderick's face, press firmly, and leave the rest to him. I'll guarantee that in something under three seconds the idea will have dawned on him that you are not required in this family." ("The Rummy Affair of Old Biffy")*

72. *"I am rather pinning my faith on the Luminous Rabbit, Jeeves. I hear excellent reports of it on all sides. You wind it up and put it in somebody's room in the night watches, and it shines in the dark and jumps about, making odd, squeaking noises the while." ("The Ordeal of Young Tuppy")*
Another episode in the campaign of vengeance sworn by Bertram Wilberforce Wooster against Hildebrand ("Tuppy") Glossop, for the occasion when, having bet that Bertie could not swing himself across the Drones swimming bath by the ropes and rings, the foul Glossop looped the last ring back, thus soaking an impeccable suit of evening dress. Cf. #67, supra: those who know Bertram Wooster best will note that the vengeance motif emerges forcibly in conjunction with the Yule-tide Spirit, so hallowed and so gracious is the time.

73. *The high point of Lord Emsworth's formative years, when Lady Constance spots the substitution for a collar stud.* Passim.

74. *Uncle Fred, Lord Ickenham's Great Sponge Joyeuse.* Passim.

75. *Isn't going to win the Waterloo Cup.* (*"The Level Business Head"*)

OLD FATHER TIME

W*hat happened...*

1. The year Martingale won the Gold Cup?

2. The year Bluebottle won the Cambridgeshire?

3. In the autumn of the year Yorkshire Pudding won the Manchester November Handicap? [* *]

4. One afternoon the year Billy Buttons won the Jubilee Cup? [* * *]

5. In the year Bingo had a bad Goodwood?

6. On 15 October 1881?

7. At the York and Ainsty Hunt Ball of 1921? [* *]

8. On 6 December 1944?

9. On 1 January 1975?

10. On St. Valentine's Day, 1975?

ANSWERS

CHAPTER V · OLD FATHER TIME

1. *Sir Gregory Parsloe and the Prawns.* (Heavy Weather)

2. *Aunt Dahlia married Thomas Portarlington Travers.* (Passim)

3. *"If ever a bird was sitting on top of the world, that bird was Bingo."* (*"Jeeves and the Old School Chum"*)

4. *Galahad Threepwood formed a friendship with a charming pea and thimble man at Hurst Park.* (Sunset at Blandings, Ch. 4)

5. *Ocean Breeze was so far behind that he nearly came in first in the next race, and Bingo whizzed off silently into the unknown. Actually, to Twing, where the Great Sermon Handicap takes place a few weeks later.* (*"Comrade Bingo," "The Great Sermon Handicap"*)

6. *P.G. Wodehouse was born, Guildford, Surrey.*

7. *"And now the gentleman in the burnous has started tickling my ankle—a thing that hasn't happened to me since the York and Ainsty Hunt Ball of the year 1921," Aunt Dahlia recollects.* (The Code of the Woosters)

8. *Wodehouse exonerated by Foreign Minister Anthony Eden in House of Commons.*

9. *Wodehouse knighted by Queen Elizabeth II*

10. *Wodehouse dies.*

PURLOINED LETTERS

R ichard Usborne has said it can't be done, and I believe him. To spot all of the quotations, displaced or submerged allusions, mangled references and literary thefts in Wodehouse would defy even the computer, which, after all, has to be fed. But let's try our hand at a few. I'll give you the original line, phrase, name or nifty, and you place it in the Wodehouse canon.

1. O Woman! in our hours of ease,
   Uncertain, coy, and hard to please,
   And variable as the shade
   By the light quivering aspen made;
   When pain and anguish wring the brow,
   A ministering angel thou!
   —Sir Walter Scott, *Marmion*

2. I strove with none, for none was worth my strife;
   Nature I loved, and next to Nature, Art.
   I warm'd both hands against the fire of life;
   It sinks, and I am ready to depart.
   —Walter Savage Landor, "Dying Speech of an Old
   Philosopher."

3. The female of the species is more deadly than the male.
   —Rudyard Kipling

4. And a woman is only a woman, but a good cigar is a smoke.
   —Rudyard Kipling, "The Betrothed"

5. The floor of heaven
    Is thick inlaid with pattens of bright gold.
    There's not the smallest orb that thou beholdest
    But in his motion like an angel sings,
    Still quiring to the young-eyed Cherubim.
    —Shakespeare, *The Merchant of Venice*

6. An eye like Mars, to threaten and command.
    —Shakespeare, *Hamlet*

7. Lo! the poor Indian, whose untutored mind
    Sees God in clouds, or hears him in the wind.
    —Alexander Pope, *An Essay on Man,* I.3

    Then must you speak
    Of one that loved not wisely, but too well;
    Of one not easily jealous, but, being wrought,
    Perplexed in the extreme; of one whose hand,
    Like the base Indian, threw a pearl away
    Richer than all his tribe.
    —Shakespeare, *Othello,* V.ii

    There used to be a poem when I learnt lessons, something
    about Lo the poor Indian whose something mind!
    —Dickens, *Little Dorrit,* Book I, Chapter 20

8. Or ever the knightly years were gone
        With the old world to the grave
    I was a King in Babylon
        And you were a Christian Slave.
    —William Ernest Henley, "To W.A."

9. The lark's on the wing;
    The snail's on the thorn;
    God's in his heaven—
    All's right with the world!
    —Robert Browning, *Pippa Passes*

10. Fly like the youthful hart or roe
    Over the hills where spices grow.
    —Isaac Watts, *Hymns and Spiritual Songs*

11. Wouldst thou have that
    Which thou esteem'st the ornament of life,
    And live a coward in thine own esteem,
    Letting "I dare not" wait upon "I would,"
    Like the poor cat i' the adage?
    —Shakespeare, *Macbeth*, I.vii

12. Look here, upon this picture, and on this,
    The counterfeit presentment of two brothers.
    —Shakespeare, Hamlet, III.iv

13. Punch, brothers, punch with care,
    Punch in the presence of the passenjare.
    —Noah Brooks (1830-1903)

14. He was a verray, parfit, gentil knight.
    —Chaucer, *Canterbury Tales*, General Prologue

15. She never told her love,
    But let concealment, like a worm i' the bud
    Feed on her damask cheek. She pined in thought;
    And, with a green and yellow melancholy,
    She sat like Patience on a monument,
    Smiling at grief.
    —Shakespeare, *Twelfth Night*

16. Oh! Ah!
    —Dickens, *Dombey and Son*, Chapter 14

17. The Assyrian came down like the wolf on the fold,
    And his cohorts were gleaming in purple and gold.
    —George Gordon, Lord Byron, "The Destruction of
    Sennacherib"

18. I could a tale unfold whose lightest word
    Would harrow up thy soul, freeze thy young blood,
    Make thy two eyes, like stars, start from their spheres,
    Thy knotted and combined locks to part
    And each particular hair to stand an end
    Like quills upon the fretful porpentine.
    —Shakespeare, *Hamlet*, I.v

19. I grant you I was down, and out of breath, and so was he;
    but we rose both at an instant and fought a long hour by
    Shrewsbury clock.
    —Shakespeare, *Henry IV Part I*, V.iv

20. Why don't you speak for yourself, John?
    —Henry Wadsworth Longfellow, "The Courtship of
    Miles Standish"

21. A Sensitive Plant in a garden grew,
    And the young winds fed it with silver dew. [* * *]
    —Percy Bysshe Shelley, "The Sensitive Plant"

22. Rem acu tetigisti.
    —Lucretius, *De Rerum Natura*

23. Then felt I like some watcher of the skies
       When a new planet swims into his ken;
    Or like stout Cortez when with eagle eyes
       He stared at the Pacific—and all his men
    Looked at each other with a wild surmise—
       Silent, upon a peak in Darien.
    —John Keats, "On First Looking into Chapman's
    Homer"

24. O Mary, go and call the cattle home,
    And call the cattle home,
    And call the cattle home,
    Across the sands o' Dee.
    —Charles Kingsley, "The Sands of Dee"

25. Abou Ben Adhem (may his tribe increase!)
    Awoke one night from a deep dream of peace.
    —Leigh Hunt, "Abou Ben Adhem"

26. All flesh is grass.
    —Isaiah, XL.6

27. Don't ask me whether I won't take none, or whether I will,
    but leave the bottle on the chimley piece, and let me put my
    lips to it when I am so dispoged.
    —Dickens, *Martin Chuzzlewit*, Chapter 19

28. Stand not upon the order of your going,
    But go at once.
    —Shakespeare, *Macbeth*, III.iv

29. Aequam memento rebus in arduis servare mentem.
    —Horace, *Odes*, II.iii

30. Child Rowland to the dark tower came,
    His word was still—Fie, foh, and fum,
    I smell the blood of a British man.
    —Shakespeare, *King Lear*, III.iv

    "Childe Roland to the Dark Tower Came"
    —Poem by Robert Browning

31. His sisters and his cousins whom he reckons up by dozens,
    His sisters and his cousins and his aunts.
    —W.S. Gilbert, *H.M.S. Pinafore*

32. These are deep waters, Watson.
    —A. Conan Doyle, *Adventures of Sherlock Holmes*,
    passim.

33. I never nursed a dear gazelle
    To glad me with its soft black eye,
    But when it came to know me well
    And love me it was sure to die.
    —Thomas Moore, *Lalla Rookh*

34. O, beware, my lord, of jealousy!
    It is the green-eyed monster, which doth mock
    The meat it feeds on.
    —Shakespeare, *Othello*, III.iii

35. She walks in beauty, like the night
    Of cloudless climes and starry skies;
    And all that's best of dark and bright
    Meet in her aspect and her eyes.
    —George Gordon, Lord Byron, "She Walks in
    Beauty"

36. Madam, I go with all convenient speed.
    —Shakespeare, *The Merchant of Venice*, III.iv

37. Though every prospect pleases, and only man is vile.
    —Reginald Heber, "Missionary Hymn"

38. A kiss for the boofer lady.
    —Dickens, *Our Mutual Friend,* Book 2, Chapter 9

39. A Daniel come to judgment! Yea, a Daniel!
    —Shakespeare, *The Merchant of Venice,*

40. Let me have men about me that are fat,
    Sleek-headed men, and such as sleep a-nights.
    —Shakespeare, *Julius Caesar.* I.ii

41. We have heard the chimes at midnight, Justice Shallow.
    —Shakespeare, *Henry IV Part II,* III.ii

42. Only this and nothing more.
    —Edgar Allan Poe, "The Raven"

43. And cast ye the unprofitable servant into outer darkness:
    there shall be weeping and gnashing of teeth.

44. *Exit, pursued by a bear.*
    —Shakespeare, *The Winter's Tale,* III.iii

45. You did not come,
    And marching Time drew on, and wore me numb. [* * *]
    —Thomas Hardy, "A Broken Appointment"

46. Shadrach, Meshach, and Abed-nego fell down bound into
    the midst of the burning fiery furnace.
    —*Daniel,* III.23

47. Two souls with but a single thought,
    Two hearts that beat as one.

    (Zwei Seelen und ein Gedanke,
    Zwei Herzen und ein Schlag.)
    —Von Münch Bellinghausen, *Ingomar the Barbarian*

48. The rank is but the guinea's stamp,
    The man's the gowd for a' that.
    —Robert Burns, "Is There for Honest Poverty"

49. Two stern-faced men set out from Lynn
     through the cold and heavy mist,
 And Eugene Aram walked between
     with gyves upon his wrist.
          —Thomas Hood, "The Dream of Eugene Aram"

50. O for a beaker full of the warm South,
     Full of the true, the blushful Hippocrene,
 With beaded bubbles winking at the brim.
          —John Keats, "Ode to a Nightingale"

51. The toad beneath the harrow knows
     Exactly where each tooth-point goes.
          —Rudyard Kipling, "Pagett, M.P."

52. Hers is the head upon which all the ends of the world are
 come, and the eyelids are a little weary.
          —Walter Pater, *Leonardo da Vinci*

53. Now fades the glimmering landscape on the sight,
     And all the air a solemn stillness holds.
          —Thomas Gray, "Elegy in a Country Churchyard"

54. He holds him with his glittering eye—
 The Wedding-Guest stood still.
          —Samuel Taylor Coleridge, "The Rime of the
          Ancient Mariner"

55. The quality of mercy is not strain'd,
     It droppeth as the gentle rain from heaven
     Upon the place beneath. It is twice bless'd;
     It blesseth him that gives and him that takes.
          —Shakespeare, *The Merchant of Venice,* IV.i

56. And thus the native hue of resolution
     Is sicklied o'er with the pale cast of thought,
     And enterprises of great pitch and moment
     With this regard their currents turn awry,
     And lose the name of action.
          —Shakespeare, *Hamlet,* III.i

57. Tired nature's sweet restorer, balmy sleep!
          —Edward Young, "Night Thoughts"

58. Not with dreams, but with blood and with iron,
    Shall a nation be moulded to last.
    —Algernon Charles Swinburne, "A Word for the
       Country"

59. His life was gentle, and the elements
    So mix'd in him that Nature might stand up
    And say to all the world, "This was a man!"
    —Shakespeare, *Julius Caesar*, V.v

60. My strength is as the strength of ten
    Because my heart is pure.
    —Alfred, Lord Tennyson, "Sir Galahad"

61. Oh, young Lochinvar is come out of the West,
    Through all the wide border his steed was the best.
    —Sir Walter Scott, *Marmion*, Canto V

62. If it were done when 'tis done, then 'twere well
    It were done quickly.
    —Shakespeare, *Macbeth*, I.vii

63. There is a tide in the affairs of men,
    Which, taken at the flood, leads on to fortune.
    —Shakespeare, *Julius Caesar*, IV.iii

64. 'Forward the Light Brigade! '
    Was there a man dismay'd?
    Not tho' the soldier knew
       Someone had blundered.
    —Alfred, Lord Tennyson, "The Charge of the
       Light Brigade"

65. In the fell clutch of circumstance,
    I have not winced nor cried aloud:
    Under the bludgeonings of chance
    My head is bloody, but unbowed.
    —William Ernest Henley, "Invictus"

66. Weave a circle round him thrice,
    And close your eyes with holy dread,
    For he on honey-dew hath fed,
    And drunk the milk of Paradise.
    —Samuel Taylor Coleridge, "Kubla Khan"

67. She starts, —she moves, —she seems to feel
    The thrill of life along her keel!
    　　—Henry Wadsworth Longfellow, "The Building
    　　　of the Ship"

68. Even the weariest river
    Winds somewhere safe to sea.
    　　—Algernon Charles Swinburne, "The Garden of
    　　　Proserpine"

69. Like one that on a lonesome road
    Doth walk in fear and dread,
    And having once turned round, walks on,
    And turns no more his head;
    Because he knows a frightful fiend
    Doth close behind him tread.
    　　—Samuel Taylor Coleridge, "The Rime of the
    　　　Ancient Mariner"

70. Life is real! Life is earnest!
    And the grave is not its goal;
    Dust thou art, to dust returnest,
    Was not spoken of the soul.
    　　—Henry Wadsworth Longfellow, "A Psalm of Life"

71. Season of mists and mellow fruitfulness,
    Close bosom-friend of the maturing sun.
    　　—John Keats, "To Autumn"

72. Between the acting of a dreadful thing
    And the first motion, all the interim is
    Like a phantasma, or a hideous dream:
    The genius and the mortal instruments
    Are then in council; and the state of man,
    Like to a little kingdom, suffers then
    The nature of an insurrection.
    　　—Shakespeare, *Julius Caesar,* II.i

73. Heaven has no rage like love to hatred turned,
    Nor hell a fury like a woman scorned.
    　　—William Congreve, *The Mourning Bride,* III.viii

74. He either fears his fate too much,
      Or his deserts are small,
    That dares not put it to the touch
      To gain or lose it all.
        —James Graham, First Marquess of Montrose,
          "My Dear and Only Love"

75. Sudden a thought came like a full-blown rose,
    Flushing his brow, and in his pained heart
    Made purple riot.
        —John Keats, "The Eve of Saint Agnes"

76. One morn a Peri at the gate
    Of Eden stood disconsolate.
        —Thomas Moore, "Paradise and the Peri

77. 'Twas on a summer's evening, in his tent,
    That day he overcame the Nervii.
        —Shakespeare, *Julius Caesar,* III.ii

78. Et ego in Arcadia vixi.
        —Motto, used by Nicolas Poussin (1594-1665) for his
          painting *Les Bergers d'Arcadie*

79. And like the baseless fabric of this vision,
    The cloud-capp'd towers, the gorgeous palaces,
    The solemn temples, the great globe itself,
    Yea, all which it inherit, shall dissolve,
    And, like this insubstantial pageant faded,
    Leave not a rack behind."
        —Shakespeare, *The Tempest,* IV.i

80. Can'st thou not minister to a mind diseas'd,
    Pluck from the memory a rooted sorrow,
    Raze out the written troubles of the brain,
    And with some sweet oblivious antidote
    Cleanse the stuff'd bosom of that perilous stuff
    Which weighs upon the heart?
        —Shakespeare, *Macbeth,* V.iii

81. Spare us the bitter pain
    Of stern denials,
    Nor with lowborn disdain
    Augment our trials.
    Hearts just as pure and fair
    May beat in Belgrave Square
    As in the lowly air
    Of Seven Dials.
        —W.S. Gilbert, "Spurn Not the Nobly Born," *Iolanthe*,
        Act I

82. For of all sad words of tongue or pen,
    The saddest are these: 'It might have been!'
        —John Greenleaf Whittier, "Maud Muller"

ANSWERS

CHAPTER VI · PURLOINED LETTERS

1. *"Remember the feller who said that women were gosh-awful pains in the neck when things were going right with you, but turned into bally angels when yer had a hangover?"*
    — Something Fishy, *Chapter 15*.

    Jeeves misquotes "rack" as "wring" in "The Spot of Art," but gets it right elsewhere.
        — Passim.

"Pigeonhole the poet Scott for a moment, or I shall be losing the thread of my remarks."
— The Mating Season, *Chapter 27.*

"You know what girls are. A tiff occurs, and they shoot their heads off. But underneath it all the old love still remains. Am I correct?"
"Quite correct, sir. The poet Scott—"
"Right-ho, Jeeves."
"Very good, sir."
— Right Ho, Jeeves, *Chapter 13.*

2. *"You are leaving Shipley Hall, sir?"*
"I am. It stinks, and I am ready to depart."
— Something Fishy, *Chapter 25.*

3. *"I've said it before, and I'll say it again—girls are rummy. Old Pop Kipling never said a truer word than when he made that crack about the f. of the s. being more d. than the m."*
— Right Ho, Jeeves, *Chapter 19.*

4. *Story titles, in* The Clicking of Cuthbert *and* Plum Pie.

5. *"Above, in the serene sky, the stars quiring to the cherubins."*
— The Mating Season, *Chapter 24;* Joy in the Morning, *Ch. 14*

6. *"Forceful is correct. What's that thing of Shakespeare's about having an eye like Mother's?"*
— The Mating Season, *Chapter 8;* passim.

7. *"Not since the historic occasion when Lo, the poor Indian, threw the pearl away, richer than all his tribe, and suddenly found out what an ass he had made of himself, had anyone experienced such remorse as now seared Adrian Peake."*
— Summer Moonshine, *Chapter XVIII*

8. *"All that in the poem, you know. How does it go? 'When you were a tiddley-om-pom, and I was a thingummajig.' Dashed brainy bit of work. I was reading it only the other day."*
— The Intrusion of Jimmy, *Chapter XXVIII.* Passim.

9. Something Fresh, *Chapter 5*. The Mating Season, *Chapter 7*.
   "God, the way she looked at it, was in His heaven and all right with the world, and it seemed to her that something ought to be done about it."
   — *"Feet of Clay"*

10. *"And Doctor Watts, who, watching one of his drives from the tee, jotted down the following couplet on the back of his score card."*
    — The Heart of a Goof, *Preface*

    Also Uncle Fred, passim.

11. *"A marked coldness of the feet, was there not? I recollect you saying that he was letting—what was it?—letting something do something. Cats entered into it, if I am not mistaken."*
    — Right Ho, *Jeeves, Chapter 1.*
    — Jeeves and the Feudal Spirit, *Chapt. 14.* Passim.

12. *"Look on this picture and on that—the one romantic, the other not . . . Eh?"*
    — *"The Spot of Art"*

13. *"Pack, Jeeves, pack with care. Pack in the presence of the passenjare."*
    — *"The Ordeal of Young Tuppy"*

    Inspired by a notice to conductors, posted in New York horsecars, this remarkable verse was published in Mark Twain's Literary Nightmare *(1876), whence, presumably, it caught (or cuffed) Wodehouse's ear. Having wondered what the allusion was for about fifteen years, I found out only when O.B. Davis, Chairman of English at Kent School, casually dropped the refrain in a Department Meeting. I goggled like an ostrich at a brass doorknob. Of course, Bartlett had it all along.*

14. *"Being myself more the parfait gentle knight, if you know what I mean, I am in grave danger of getting the short end."*
    — *"The Spot of Art"*

15. *"Like Patience, as you very shrewdly remark, on a monument. So we must cluster round."*
    — Jeeves and the Song of Songs"

16. *"The spectacle drew from me a quick "Oh, ah," for I was somewhat embarrassed."*
    — Right Ho, Jeeves, *Chapter 19.*

'Responding with a brief "Oh, ah," I gave my attention to the butler, who was endeavoring to communicate something to me."
— The Code of the Woosters, *Chapter 2.* Passim.

17. *"He was once more in the position of an Assyrian fully licensed to come down like a wolf on the fold with his cohorts all gleaming with purple and gold."*
— *Jeeves and the Feudal Spirit, Chapter 15*

18. *"Knitted socks and porcupines entered into it, I remember."*
— Jeeves in the Offing, *Chapter 11*

"I have a story to relate which I think you will agree falls into the fretful porpentine class."
— *Ibid., Chapter 20.*

Galahad at Blandings, *Chapter 3.* — Passim.

Joy in the Morning, *Chapter 20.* — Passim.

19. *"I've been hanging on to this damned receiver a long hour by Shrewsbury clock."*
— Jeeves in the Offing, *Chapter 6. Also 7, 10.*

"But he could not have sold this piece of philosophy to Lord Tilbury at this point in his career if he had argued with him a full hour by Shrewsbury clock."
— Biffen's Millions, *Chapter 9*

20. Money for Nothing, *Chapter IV.*

21. *"I remembered something Jeeves had once called Gussie. 'A sensitive plant, what?'*
" 'Exactly. You know your Shelley, Bertie.' "
" 'Oh, am I?' "
— The Code of the Woosters, *Chapter 3*

22. *"Precisely, madam."*
— Jeeves and the Feudal Spirit, *Chapters 12, 19,* passim.

23. *"No one was more keenly alive than I to the fact that one such bone was scheduled to make its debut the instant I swam into his ken."*
— Jeeves and the Feudal Spirit, *Chapter 1.*

"He looked at her with what I have heard Jeeves call a wild surmise."
— Jeeves in the Offing, *Chapter 7.* Passim.

24. *Aunt Dahlia could make a good living at it.*
— *"Jeeves and the Song of Songs,"* et passim.

25. *"Who was the chap, lo! whose name led all the rest—the bird with the angel?"*
— The Code of the Woosters, *Chapter 5; "How's That, Umpire?"*

"Abu had clicked, and Lord Biskerton expected to click."
— Big Money, *Ch. 13*

26. The Code of the Woosters, *Chapter 5*

27. *"You mean she's actually got the stuff in the bank, where she can lay hands on it whenever she feels disposed?"*
— *"Feet of Clay"*

28. *"He stood not upon the order of going but immediately soared over the rail and plunged into the water below."*
— *"Tangled Hearts"*

29. Biffen's Millions, *Chapter 9*

30. *"Childe Roland to the dark tower came, sir,"* said Jeeves, as we alighted, though what he meant I hadn't an earthly."*
— The Code of the Woosters, *Chapter 2.*

"I squared the shoulders and strode to the door, like Childe Roland about to fight the Paynim."
— The Mating Season, *Chapter 27.*

31. *"The word flies round the family circle that you're a good provider, and up roll all the sisters and cousins and aunts and nephews and uncles to stake out their claims, several being injured in the crush."*
— Jeeves and the Feudal Spirit, *Chapter 1.*

32. *"These are deep waters, Jeeves."*
— Ibid.

33. *"Round about the beginning of July each year he downs tools, the slacker, and goes off to Bognor Regis for the shrimping, leaving me in much the same position as those poets one used to have to read at school who were always beefing about losing gazelles.*
— Ibid.

34. *"Ever since then the green-eyed monster has always been more or less round and about, ready to snap into action at the drop of a hat . . . ."*

    "And Stilton, of course, as I have already indicated, is a chap who could give Othello a couple of bisques and be dormy one at the eighteenth."
    — Ibid. Chapter 2.

35. *" 'She walks in beauty like the night of cloudless climes and starry skies; and all that's best of dark and bright meet in her aspect and her eyes. Another bit of bread and cheese,' he said to the lad behind the bar."*
    — "The Pride of the Woosters is Wounded"

36. *" 'Do so, Jeeves,' I said proudly, 'and with all convenient speed.' "*
    — "Jeeves and the Yuletide Spirit"

37. *"Totleigh Towers might be a place where Man was vile, but undoubtedly every prospect pleased."*

38. *"And we must get a good line for the child. 'Boofer lady, does 'oo love dadda?' isn't definite enough."*
    — "Fixing It for Freddie"

39. *"Tipton eyed him reverently. A Daniel come to judgment, he was feeling."*
    — Galahad at Blandings, *Chapter 1*

40 *"Julius Caesar, who liked to have men about him that were fat, would have taken to him at once."*
    — Ibid.

41. *"As many people did, he had taken an instant liking to this son of one with whom he had so often heard the chimes of midnight."*
    — Ibid., *Chapter 3*

42. Something Fresh, *Chapter 2: "R. JONES,"* simply that and nothing more.

43. *"It may be that this vigil in a broken-down car will cause Rosie to see what you'd have thought she ought to have seen years ago—viz: that the Pyke is entirely unfit for human consumption and must be cast into outer darkness where there is wailing and gnashing of teeth."*
    — "Jeeves and the Old School Chum"

44. *"I remember drawing a picture of it on the side of the page, when I was at school."*
    — *"Indian Summer of an Uncle"*

45. *"The clock ticked on, but she did not come."*
    — *"The Spot of Art"*

46. *"The mere sight of them gave me the sort of feeling Shadrach, Meshach and Abednego must have had when preparing to enter the burning, fiery furnace.*
    — *"Jeeves and the Song of Songs"*

47. *"What was it the poet said of couples like the Bingeese?"*
    " 'Two minds with but a single thought, two hearts that beat as one,' sir."
    "A dashed good description, Jeeves."
    — *"Jeeves and the Old School Chum"*

48. *"All right, guinea stamp. Though I don't believe there is such a thing. I shouldn't have thought they came higher than five bob."*
    — *"Indian Summer of an Uncle"*

49. *" 'A little trouble last night with the minions of the Law, Jeeves,' I said. 'Quite a bit of that Eugene-Aram-walked-between-with-gyves-upon-his-wrists stuff.' "*
    — Jeeves and the Feudal Spirit, *Chapter 6*

50. *"And while the blushful Hippocrene of which she had just imbibed her share had been robust and full of inner meaning, it had obviously merely scratched the surface."*
    — Ibid, *Chapter 12*

    "Oh, I was saying to myself, for a beaker full of the warm South, full of the true, the blushful Hippocrene."
    — The Mating Season, *Chapter 23*. Passim.

51. *"Well, if I met the Mona Lisa at this moment, I would shake her by the hand and assure her that I know just how she felt. You see before you, Jeeves, a toad beneath the harrow."*
    — The Code of the Woosters, *Chapter 5*

    "You see before you a man who is as near to being what is known as a toad at Harrow as a man can be who was educated at Eton."
    — Aunts Aren't Gentlemen, *Chapter 14*

52. *"The Mona Lisa, sir."*
    — The Code of the Woosters, *Chapter 5*

53. *"Well, Jeeves got off a good one the other day. I met him airing the dog in the park one evening, and he said, 'Now fades the glimmering landscape on the sight, sir, and all the air a solemn stillness holds.' You might use that."*
    — Right Ho, *Jeeves, Chapter 9*

    * *By the way . . . what dog?*

54. *"Her eye, swiveling round, stopped me like a bullet. The Wedding Guest, if you remember, had the same trouble with the Ancient Mariner."*
    — The Mating Season, *Chapter 21*

55. *"You mean it droppeth as the gentle rain from Heaven?"*
    "Precisely, sir. Upon the place beneath."
    — Ibid., *Chapter 8*
    Jeeves in the Offing, *Chapt. 20.* Passim.

56. *"His brow was sicklied o'er with the pale cast of thought and his air was that of a man who, if he had said 'hullo, girls,' would have said it like someone in a Russian drama announcing that Grandpapa had hanged himself in the barn."*
    — Ibid., *Chapter 2*

57. *"What was it I heard you call sleep the other day, Jeeves?"*
    — Ibid., *Chapter 4*

58. *"And you didn't quail? You must have been a child of blood and iron."*
    — Ibid., *Chapter 8*

59. *" 'Completely, Orlo. His life is gentle, and the elements mixed in him just right,' I said, remembering a gag of Jeeves's."*
    — Aunts Aren't Gentlemen, *Chapter 17*

    "I always remember that bit. Had to write it out a hundred times at school for bunging an orange at a contemporary and catching my form-master squarely in the eyeball."
    — Big Money, *Chapter 13*

60. *"I remember Jeeves once speaking of someone of his acquaintance whose strength was as the strength of ten, and the description would have fitted Stilton nicely."*
   — Jeeves and the Feudal Spirit, Chapter 3, 11

61. *"Who could say that the latter, finding me in residence on his arrival, would not leap to the conclusion that I had rolled up in pursuit of the former like young Lochinvar coming out of the west?"*
   — Ibid., Chapter 8

62. " *'If it were . . . what's that expression of yours?'*
   " *'If it were done when 'tis done, then 'twere well it were done quickly, sir.'*
   " *'That's right. No sense in standing humming and hawing.'*

63. " *'No, sir. There is a tide in the affairs of men which, taken at the flood, leads on to fortune.*
   " *'Exactly,' I said."*
   — Ibid., Chapter 12.

64. *"The thing goes, as you probably know,*
   Tum tiddle umpty-pum
   Tum tiddle umpty-pum
   Tum tiddle umpty-pum
   and this brought you to the snapperoo or pay-off, which was
   Someone had blundered."
   — Ibid., Chapter 13.

65. *"Under the tiddly-poms of whatever-it-is . . . How does the rest of it go?"*
   — Ibid., Chapter 14

66. *"Her whole aspect was that of an aunt who on honeydew has fed and drunk the milk of Paradise, and the thought crossed my mind that if she was feeling as yeasty as this before hearing the good news, she might quite easily, when I spilled same, explode with a loud report."*
   — Ibid., Chapter 18

67. *"I remember when I was a kid at school having to learn a poem of sorts about a fellow named Pig-something—a sculptor he would have been, no doubt—who made a statute of a girl, and what should happen one morning but that the bally thing suddenly came to life."*
   — Right Ho, Jeeves, Chapter 9

*The lines Bertie then quotes are from Longfellow's "The Building of the Ship," nothing to do with Pygmalion at all.

"The impression prevailing among the gnats, moths and beetles which had accompanied him on the home stretch was that he had been turned into a pillar of salt, and it came as a great surprise to them when at the end of perhaps five minutes he moved and stirred and seemed to feel the rush of life along his keel."
— A Pelican at Blandings, Chapter 7

68. "Even the weariest river winds somewhere to the sea. With a moving period, the butler finally concluded his narrative."
— Leave it to Psmith, Chapter IX

69. "As a matter of fact, the frightful fiend had given up the pursuit after the first few steps, and a moment later I drew this fact to Ukridge's attention, for it was not the sort of day on which to break walking records unnecessarily."
— "Ukridge's Dog College"

70. "Life is stern and life is earnest, and if I mean to make a fortune I've got to bustle about and not stay cooped up in a place like Wimbledon . . . . Besides which, [my aunt] told me the very sight of me made her sick and she never wanted to see me again."
— Ibid.

71. "There is a fog, sir. If you will recollect, we are now in Autumn—season of mists and mellow fruitfulness."
— The Code of the Woosters, Chapter 1

72. "I explain this to Jeeves, and he said that much the same thing had bothered Hamlet."
— Joy in the Morning, Chapter XXI

* True enough: much the same thing did bother Hamlet; but the lines Jeeves quotes here describe the same thing bothering **Brutus**. As Bertie says, "He puts these things well"—and rarely makes this sort of bloomer.

73. "I remember Jeeves saying on one occasion—I forget how the subject had arisen—he may simply have thrown the observation out, as he does sometimes, for me to take or leave—that hell hath no fury like a woman scorned."
— Right Ho, Jeeves, Chapter XXIII

74. *"On the face of the Hon. Freddie, as he advanced into the room, there was that set, grim expression which is always seen on the faces of those who are about to put their fortune to the test, to win or lose it all."*
    — *"The Go-Getter"*

    "On a score of previous occasions T. Paterson Frisby had contemplated laying his widowed heart at the feet of this woman, of putting his fortune to the test, to win or lose it all; but always he had refrained."
    — Big Money, *Chapter 11.*
    Elsewhere, passim.

75. *"Suddenly a thought came like a full-blown rose, flushing his brow; and, charging downstairs to the cellar, he came racing up again, armed now with the pick-axe used by suburban householders for breaking coal."*
    — Big Money, *Chapter 13*

76. *"There is a certain point past which you cannot push the freemen of Valley Fields. That point, he now realized, had been reached when he had closed the morning-room window, leaving the cloth-capped man standing outside like a Peri at the gates of Paradise."*
    — Big Money, *Chapter 6*

77. *"The makings were neatly laid out on a side-table, and to pour into a glass an inch or so of the raw spirit and shoosh some soda-water on top of it was with me the work of a moment. This done, I retired to an arm-chair and put my feet up, sipping the mixture with carefree enjoyment, rather like Caesar having one in his tent the day he overcame the Nervii."*
    — Right Ho, Jeeves, *Chapter 11*

    "I met her once, Jeeves. T'was on a summer's evening in my tent, the day I overcame the Nervii. Or, rather, at lunch at Aunt Agatha's a year ago come Lammas Eve. It is not an experience I would willingly undergo again."
    — *"Jeeves and the Kid Clementina"*

78. *"Once he, also, had lived in Arcady and thrown bread at Old Boys' dinners."*
    — Big Money, *Chapter 7*

    See also Uncle Fred, passim.

79. *" 'Jeeves,' I yelled.*
"But he had gone, leaving not a wrack behind."
— The Code of the Woosters, *Chapter 5*
Jeeves in the Offing, *Chapter 7,* et passim.

* A rack—or wrack—is a wisp of cloud.

80. *"I cleansed my bosom of a good deal of that perilous stuff that weighs upon the heart."*
— *"First Aid for Dora"*

"And Henry, having cleansed his stuff'd bosom of that perilous stuff which weighs upon the heart, shoved the stick energetically once more through the railings."
— Jill the Reckless, *Chapter 5*

81. *"Hearts, the policeman knew, just as pure and fair may beat in Belgrave square as in the lowlier air of Seven Dials, but you have to pinch them just the same."*
— Jill the Reckless, *Chapter 5*

82. *"Of all sad words of tongue or pen, the saddest are these—'He knew something good, but could not make a touch.' "*
— Big Money, *Chapter 12;* passim.

BIBLIOGRAPHICA

1. What first edition is imprinted "P.J. Wodehouse" on the spine?

2. What first edition misspells Wodehouse's middle name on the copyright page? [* *]

3. What first edition has the title of another book on the ½-title page? [* *]

4. What author dedicated what book to what Wodehouse character? [* * *]

5. What book is dedicated to cousins of H.M. the Queen Mother?

6. To whom, in what novel, is Wodehouse's longest dedication?

7. What book did Wodehouse dedicate "Ad Matrem," and what does that mean?

8. Wodehouse wrote a play which he then turned into a short novel which was published in America in a collection of stories. What are the three titles?

9. Page 31, line 12, of what first edition misprints "friend potatoes" for "fried potatoes"?

10. What famous *New Yorker* artist did the dust wrapper for what book by Wodehouse?

11. What was Wodehouse's first full-length novel?

12. What was Wodehouse's first full-length novel for adults?

13. What novel appeared first under its first title in the U.S., then as a different story under a different title in England, then as yet a third different story under its original title in England?

14. What is the novel which, though listed for years by both Doubleday and Simon & Schuster as *White Hope*, was never actually published as a book under that title . . . though it *was* published in serial form under that title in Munsey's Magazine?

15. What is the only prose fiction title under which PGW shares a by-line?

16. What is the only other prose title under which he shares a by-line?

17. What is the book with verses, not by PGW, between chapters?

18. In what dedication is the name of the recipient misspelled?

19. Without the help of that same recipient, PGW in another dedication claims, he would have finished the book in half the time. Who? What book?

20. In "Bramley Is So Bracing," Freddie Widgeon refers to an author, who dedicated a book to P.G. Wodehouse. Who is the author, and what is the title of the book?

21. What is the incidental joke concerning the well-known American artist and her portrait of the Empress for the dust wrapper of the Doubleday, Doran edition of *Uncle Fred in the Springtime*?

22. What is the short story which has been published twice as a separate volume . . . and is going on to more in other languages?

23. In the first sentence of what American first edition is there an obvious typographical error which does not occur in the English edition of the same title? [* * * *]

24. In what Jeeves story, in what edition, does Wodehouse give Aunt Agatha's butler two different names, once on the same page?

25. Apart from Madeline Bassett's fondness for his works—where does Wodehouse make scantily veiled mockery of A.A. Milne?

ANSWERS

CHAPTER VII · BIBLIOGRAPHICA

1. Biffen's Millions: *Simon & Schuster.*

2. Big Money: *Doubleday, Doran. ("Granville")*

3. Jeeves in the Offing: *Jenkins. ("A Few Quick Ones")*

4. *William Townend dedicated* The Top Landing *to Albert Peasemarch,* "Prince of Stewards" *from* The Luck of the Bodkins.

5. The Pothunters.

6. *To Peter Schwed,* Bertie Wooster Sees it Through, *a 4-page dedication derived from a piece which appeared in* Punch *(31 March 1954). Mr. Schwed was Wodehouse's Editor and Publisher at Simon and Schuster, and devised this title for* Jeeves *and the Feudal* Spirit *(see Chapter III above).*

7. Tales of St. Austin's *is dedicated "Ad Matrem," which literally means "To Mother" but is more likely intended as a dedication to Dulwich College, Wodehouse's only true Alma Mater.*

8. Good Morning, Bill! Doctor Sally. The Medicine Girl.

9. Indiscretions of Archie: *George H. Doran.*

10. *Rea Irvin.*

11. The Pothunters.

12. Love Among the Chickens.

13. The Prince and Betty (Psmith, Journalist).

14. Their Mutual Child (The Coming of Bill).

15. Not George Washington *(with Herbert Westbrook).*

16. Bring on the Girls *(with Guy Bolton).*

17. William Tell Told Again.

18. Piccadilly Jim: *Dodd, Mead. ("Lenora")*

19. *"To my daughter, Leonora . . . ."* Divots/The Heart of A Goof

20. *E. Phillips Oppenheim:* Up the Ladder of Gold.

21. *Her name: Peggy Bacon.*

22. *"The Great Sermon Handicap."*

23. A Damsel in Distress: *George H. Doran. ("country" for "country")*

24. *In "Jeeves and the Impending Doom," p. 565 of the original Jenkins edition of the* Jeeves Omnibus. *Corrected in later issues.*

25. *"Rodney Has a Relapse," in* Nothing Serious.

OTHER AUTHORS (MATCHING 'EM ALL)

M *atch the following Writers in Wodehouse with their works:*

1. Rosie M. Banks

2. Sir Raymond (Beefy) Bastable as Richard Blunt

3. Augustus Whiffle (a.k.a. Whipple)

4. Gerald Foster

5. James Corcoran

6. Ashe Marson as Felix Clovelly

7. George Caffyn

8. P.G. Wodehouse

9. Pilkington/Trevis

10. Wally Mason

11. Wilmot Royce

12. Leila J. Pinckney

13. Adeline (Mrs. Horace) Hignet

14. Florence Craye

a. "The Adventure of the Secret Six"—A Gridley Quayle Story

b. *The Rose of America*

c. *The Primrose Way*

d. *The Stench of Life*

e. *Wodehouse on the Niblick*

f. *Offal* and *Worm i' the Root*

g. *American Birds* and *More American Birds*

h. *What Ho, Twing!*

i. *Heather O' the Hills*

j. *'Twas on an English June*

k. *The Mystery of the Severed Ear*

l. "Mother, She's Pinching my Leg"

m. *Spindrift*

n. "What the Well-Dressed Man is Wearing

15. Emily Ann Mackintosh   o. *Roses Red and Roses White*

16. Gwendolen Moon   p. *Cocktail Time*

17. John Gooch   q. *Ask Dad*

18. Clifford Gandle   r. "BE!"

19. Blair Eggleston   s. *What of Tomorrow?*

20. Horatio Slingsby   t. *Watchman, What of the Night?*

21. Mrs. Lora Delane Porter   u. *Strychnine in the Soup*

22. Rockmetteller Todd   v. *The Spreading Light*

23. Alexander Worple   w. *On the Care of the Pig*

24. Richard (Bingo) Little   x. *Only A Factory Girl*

25. Bertram Wilberforce Wooster   y. *Follow the Girl*

ANSWERS

CHAPTER VIII · OTHER AUTHORS

1 —*x*	14 —*m*
2 —*p*	15 —*o*
3 —*w*	16 —*j*
4 —*c*	17 —*k*
5 —*l*	18 —*t*
6 —*a*	19 —*f*
7 —*q*	20 —*u*
8 —*e*	21 —*s*
9 —*b*	22 —*r*
10 —*y*	23 —*g*
11 —*d*	24 —*h*
12 —*i*	25 —*n*
13 —*v*	

WHEELS WITHIN WHEELS

*F*rom *the column on the right, select the drivers or riders of the vehicles on the left. Some vehicles may claim more than one answer. Several vehicles may claim the same answer.*

A	_____	a Rolls Royce
B	_____	a Widgeon Seven
C	_____	a bicycle
D	_____	a motorcycle
E	_____	a Dex-Mayo [*]
F	_____	an Antelope [* *]
G	_____	a Buffy-Porson
H	_____	a Station Taxi
I	_____	a Bingley
J	_____	a perambulator
K	_____	a caravan
L	_____	a motor-bicycle
M	_____	a Hispano-Suiza
N	_____	a Bentley
O	_____	an AC [* *]

1. Bolt
2. Voules
3. John Carroll
4. Jno. Robinson (a.k.a. Ed)
5. Pongo Twistleton
6. Horace Pendlebury-Davenport
7. Bertie Wooster/Jeeves
8. Gwladys Pendlebury
9. Ian Hay
10. Eustace Oates
11. Mervyn Spink
12. Algernon Aubrey Little
13. Bertram Wooster, solo "on the wheel," including one appearance nude
14. P.G. Wodehouse

P _____ a Darracq
          [* * *]

15. Hugo Carmody

16. Rupert Baxter

17. Slingsby

18. Tipton Plimsoll

19. Jane Abbot

20. Chimp Twist

ANSWERS

CHAPTER IX · WHEELS WITHIN WHEELS

A *18* (Galahad at Blandings)

B *7, 8, 19*

C *13, 10*

D *11*

E *1, 3, 20*

F *2* (Fish Preferred)

G *5*

H *4*

I *6*

J *12*

K *16*

L *17*

M *2* (Fish Preferred)

N *2* (Sunset at Blandings)

O *9, 14. (See Connolly,* P.G. Wodehouse, *p. 32: often reproduced photograph)*

P *14 (See Chronology in Morgan Catalogue)*

LARGE AUSTRALIAN BIRD:

"*She looked at me like someone who has just solved the crossword puzzle with a shrewd "Emu" in the top right-hand corner.*"
—The Code of the Woosters

(CLUES ON PAGES FOLLOWING)

Across

1. Soaked by Hildebrand Glossop

7. House agent historian

15. Bertie, according to Aunt Agatha

16. Encouraging word (slang)

17. Continent where Bertie feels safe from Aunt Agatha

18. Children (slang)

20. Sippy on Boat Race Night (slang)

21. Ice ___ the Bedroom

22. Cook engaged to ex-cook named, eponymously, Hash (initials)

23. Usually good for a fiver at the Foreign Office (initials)

24. Dropped in Bottleton East

25. Cheesewright sobriquet, contracted

26. Dial for Murder (Title by one of PGW's favorites)

27. Clarence is, Galahad isn't

29. ___ -cum-spiff.

32. Bradbury Fisher travels by

34. Painting Proposed: "The Pig at ___"

35. Mrs. Tinkler-Moulke

36. Monkey business.

38. For Bertie at Twing Village Hall

40. Rich. Also an eponym.

41. Pub near Seaview Cottage (3 words)

44. Julia Ukridge travels by

45. Much ___ About Nothing (Jeeves would know)

46. Mike yearns for. Claude and Eustace sent down from.

47. 100- ___ Dash

49. "___ is life, Jeeves"

51. Emsworth sister Lady ___

52. Later Sidcup

53. A bounder and a ___

54. "___ Treatment" (story)

57. Uncle Willoughby's and Galahad's are hot, in every sense of the word

58. "___ Ol' Man River" (dial.)

59. "___ -frightfully-Ho"

60. ___ Money (novel)

61. "He's just my ___"

62. Jeeves and Bertie both, like Aunt Dahlia and Honoria Glossop—but not the same things.

63. Wodehouse Initial

64. Another Wodehouse Initial

65. ___ Prefect's Uncle (novel)

66. Concern of "The Wheat-Growers' Intelligencer and Stock-Breeders' Gazette" (abbr.)

67. Ice in the Bedroom
    (abbr.)

69. The Cohen Bros. can suit
    one to a

70. Uncle Fred disrupts (2
    words)

74. Wodehouse citizenship

75. Oldest House Member

77. The Boy Scout,
    abbreviatedly addressed

78. A quick ____. Better a
    few of them

79. "____ toad at Harrow."
    Wooster and Gould both.

80. Hard to pronounce. BBC
    allows five variations.
    Ukridge's middle name.

Down

1. After most races (4
   words)

2. The Rev. Aubrey Sellick
   is one, Aunt Dahlia
   another. Psmith was one
   once.

3. Becomes slang as
   participle. *Cf. smash.*

4. A bullet hole is put
   through Psmith's. Sir
   Roderick's is swiped.

5. Bertie leaves several
   country houses by a
   circuitous (abbr.)

6. Arnold Abney is one,
   Aubrey Upjohn is one.

7. To withdraw from a
   gaming table, in Monte
   Carlo or elsewhere,
   regardless of the soft
   shirt or the white jacket
   (4 words)

8. Bingo's uncle, among
   others, got his,
   presumably (abbr.)

9. Drivel. Urged not to talk
   it, most do.

10. Where Bertie frequents
    the same haunts his
    creator did; where Rocky
    Todd does not want to
    go at all.

11. Last name of the
    inspiration for Ukridge's
    Accident Syndicate (* *)

13. Lord Uffenham is one,
    Gally is one, sometimes
    Lord Emsworth is one;
    the Duke of Dunstable is
    not one. (4 words, the
    last one abbreviated)

14. Vicomte, Maurice de
    Blissac dines in la ____.

19. Sir Roderick is a Fellow
    of

26. Beach address his
    employer's brother as (2
    words)

28. Bertie yearns to lower one on Tuppy. Fate in PGW *always* has one to lower. (2 words)

30. Eustace Hignet doesn't marry for (2 words)

31. George, with camera, not with airgun. 3 words, the last contracted.

33. Aunt Dahlia's Sun God

37. Rory Carlyle confesses he has not read the Zend Avesta of.

39. Foremost Wodehouse Scholar (initials)

42. The King, to Bertie. The Queen, to us.

43. Since when.

48. Jno., except in one book where he is ____ . Taxi driver.

50. Bestowed upon Wodehouse a Knighthood

55. Vanringham houseboat (fig.)

56. "____ My Daughter Leonora, Queen of her Species" (*Leave it to Psmith*)

65. Aunt Dahlia is a graceful one.

66. What Pilbeam always wants (2 words)

68. Bertie plays in his sometimes, almost always declines to be disturbed in it

69. "____ Lost Lambs" (*Captain serial*)

71. Somebody Else's Bodkins. (An Elizabethan oath)

72. Napoleon at Water ____ . English euphemism for W.C., which is a euphemism too. Are they related?

73. The Emsworth Arms is one of many

75. The Heart ____ a Goof

76. She had an eye, like Mars, to threaten and command, Bertie thought. She also had, in her full title, a knee. (*)

79. Model for *Bachelors Anonymous*

CHAPTER X · LARGE AUSTRALIAN BIRD:

B	E	R	T	R	A	M	■	C	O	R	N	E	L	I	U	S
I	D	I	O	T	■	A	T	A	B	O	Y	■	U	■	N	A
N	I	P	P	E	R	S	■	L	I	T	■	I	N	■	C	L
G	T	■	H	■	S	T	I	L	T	■	M	■	T	A	L	L
O	O	J	A	H	■	E	■	I	■	R	R	■	B	E	E	
I	R	A	T	E	■	R	A	N	N	Y	G	A	Z	O	O	■
N	■	N	■	S	R	O	■	O	■	A	■	O	O	F	Y	
T	H	E	C	H	U	F	F	N	E	L	L	A	R	M	S	
H	M	S	■	O	■	A	■	E	■	A	D	O	■	U	■	
E	■	M	E	T	E	R	■	S	U	C	H	■	A	N	N	
S	P	O	D	E	■	T	I	C	K	■	A	B	S	E	N	T
O	■	N	■	M	S	S	■	H	■	D	A	T	■	Y	O	
U	N	E	A	S	Y	■	B	I	L	L	■	R	E	A	D	■
P	■	Y	■	W	■	A	■	P	■	A	G	R	■	I	B	
■	T	■	P	O	N	G	O	S	L	I	F	E	■	U	S	A
O	H	M	■	T	■	E	D	■	O	N	E	■	A	■	T	
F	E	A	T	H	E	R	S	T	O	N	E	H	A	U	G	H

A SPOT OF ART

Identify each of the Wodehouse characters pictured below.

1) _____ 2) _____

3) _____ 4) _____

5) _____ 6) _____

7) _____ 8) _____

9) _____ 10) _____

11) _____

12) _____

13) _____

14) _____

15) —————————————

16) —————————————

17) —————————————

ANSWERS

CHAPTER XI · A SPOT OF ART

1) *Mr. Mulliner*

2) *Lady Constance*

3) *Roderick Spode*

4) *Edwin the Boy Scout*

5) *Ukridge*

6) *Madeline Bassett*

7) *Anatole*

8) *Angus McAllister*

9) *Sir Roderick Glossop*

10) *Gussie Fink-Nottle*

11) *George Cyril Wellbeloved*

12) *The Hon. Galahad Threepwood*

13) *The Man with the Hoe (One of the Wrecking Crew) ("Chester Forgets Himself") (Painting by Millet)*

14) *The First Grave Digger (One of the Wrecking Crew)*

15) *Old Father Time (One of the Wrecking Crew)*

16) *Consul, the Almost Human (One of the Wrecking Crew) (C. Marius, 157-86 B.C.)*

17) *Cyril Waddesley-Davenport ("Monkey Business")*

*(Illustrations by
Peter van Straaten)*

TRUE OR FALSE?

1. The Junior Ganymede Club Book never falls into wrong hands.   T F

2. Bertram Wooster is an only child.   T F

3. Wodehouse was born on Dunraven Street, London.   T F

4. Dolly Molloy and Chimp Twist are cousins.   T F

5. Claude and Eustace are the only twins in Wodehouse.   T F

6. Bertie and Gussie are cousins.   T F

7. The Empress never loses the Fat Pig contest.   T F

8. Galahad Threepwood and Jeeves live in the same building.   T F

9. The Story of the Prawns is related, at last, in *Sunset at Blandings.*   T F

10. "Featherstonehaugh" rhymes with "pfuff."   T F

11. "Moffinghame" rhymes with "moom."   T F

12. "Mapledurham" rhymes with "mum."   T F

13. "Magdalen," at Oxford, rhymes with "mane."   T F

14. Mr. Mulliner always takes his whisky neat.   T F

15. If you stand outside Romano's in the Strand, you can see the clock on the wall of the Law Courts down in Fleet Street.   T F

16. "Wooster" rhymes with "Schuster."   T   F

17. "Towcester" is pronounced "Grille."   T   F

18. Bertie Wooster never marries.   T   F

19. Lord Emsworth re-marries, eventually, at Lady Constance's nagging.   T   F

20. At last report, Madeline Bassett is engaged to Gussie Fink-Nottle.   T   F

21. Freddie Threepwood sells cat food in America.   T   F

22. Prudence Baxter and Rupert Baxter meet at the Market Blandings Fête.   T   F

23. Lord Emsworth has a Pig Phase, a Pumpkin Phase, a Parrot Phase and a Rose Phase, but never a Scarab Phase.   T   F

24. Valerie Twistleton, Pongo's wife, is Lord Emsworth's only daughter.   T   F

25. Rosie M. Banks wrote A STIRRING REVELATION OF A YOUNG GIRL'S SOUL.   T   F

26. Sir Roderick Glossop is the only character who appears in both the Jeeves and the Blandings stories.   T   F

ANSWERS

CHAPTER XII · TRUE OR FALSE?

1. *F*   *(It falls into Bingley's*—Much Obliged, Jeeves)

2. *F*   *(He has a sister: "Bertie Changes His Mind")*

3. *F*   *(Guildford, Surrey)*

4. *F*

5. *F*   *(George and Alfred Mulliner)*

6. *F*

7. *T*

8. *T*   (A Pelican at Blandings: *Berkeley Mansions, W1*)

9. *F*

10. *F*   *(BBC Pronouncing Dictionary offers five pronunciations, ranging from what it looks like to Fanshawe. Richard Usborne told me to pronounce it phonetically, accent on the first syllable. That makes it a dactyll with an irrational syllable, or a breather.)*

11. *T*   *(It does.* Indiscretions of Archie)

12. *T*   *("Strychnine in the Soup")*

13. *F*   *(Ask any Oxford Man*—Usborne, Wimsey, Wooster)

14. *F*   *(Hot Scotch with Lemon)*

15. *T*   *(Win a Bet: "Bertie Changes His Mind")*

16. *T*   *(Probably)*

17. *F*   *("Toaster," surely)*

18. *T*   *("A double blessing is a double grace."*—Hamlet)

19. *F*   *(Gawdhelpus, No!)*

20. *F*   *(Surprised? Re-read* Stiff Upper Lip, Jeeves)

21.   *F*   *(Dog Food)*

22.   *F*

23.   *F*   *(No Parrots)*

24.   *F*   *(Pongo's sister, no relation to Lord E. at all)*

25.   *F*   *(But she might have done: see Garrison, p. 6, for The Real Jane Emmeline Banks)*

26.   *T*

ADDRESS BOOK

M atch addresses on the left with occupants on the right.

1. Rudge Hall, Rudge-in-the-Vale, Worcs.

2. 47 Charles St., W1

3. 3A, Berkeley Mansions

4. 7 Arundel Court, Leicester Square

5. Matchingham Hall

6. "Mon Repos," Burberry Road, Valley Fields SW23

7. C6 Berkeley Mansions, W1

8. 5 Dover Street

9. Bloxham Mansions, Park Lane

10. Mafeking Road, Bramley-on Sea

11. Totleigh Towers, Gloucestershire

a. Oofy Prosser

b. Mrs. Tinkler-Moulke

c. Pat Wyvern

d. Dahlia Travers

e. The Drones

f. Bertram W. Wooster

g. Thomas (Bill) Hardy

h. Aubrey Upjohn, M.A.

i. Ashe Marson

j. Sir Gregory Parsloe-Parsloe

k. Sir Roderick's fiancee, Lady Myrtle

l. Sir Watkyn Bassett

m. Aubrey Upjohn, M.A.

n. Mike and Psmith

12. Chuffnell Hall, Chuffnell Regis, Somersetshire

13. The Cedars, Wimbledon Common

14. Deverill Hall, King's Deverill, Hampshire

15. Sanstead House

16. Dreever Castle

17. Belpher Castle

18. Windles, Windlehurst, Hampshire

19. Ickenham Hall

20. Clement's Inn

21. Towcester Abbey

22. Ditteredge Hall

23. 6b, Harley Street, London W.

24. Walsingford Hall, Walsingford Parva, Berkshire

25. Hotel Cosmopolis

o. Eustace Hignett

p. Julia Ukridge

q. Daniel Brewster

r. William Egerton Bamfylde Ossingham Belfry

s. The Earl of Marshmoreton

t. Spennie

u. Uncle Fred

v. Sir Buckstone Abbott

w. Oswald Glossop

x. Five Aunts

y. Sir Roderick Glossop

ANSWERS

CHAPTER XIII · ADDRESS BOOK

A	9	N	20
B	7	O	18
C	1	P	13
D	2	Q	25
E	8	R	21
F	3	S	17
G	6	T	16
H	15	U	19
I	4	V	24
J	5	W	22
K	12	X	14
L	11	Y	23
M	10		

THE BUTLER DID IT

1. Jeeves has been in the service of   a) Lord Worplesdon
   b) Digby Thistleton   c) Montague Todd   d) a and c   e) all
   of the above

2. Vosper has been in the service of   a) Reggie Pepper   b) the
   Duke of Bootle   c) Bradbury Fisher   d) b and c   e) none of
   the above.

3. Only of late a butler, the most pestilential of servitors in the
   Wodehouse directory is   a) Augustus Keggs   b) Charlie
   Silversmith   c) Sebastian Beach   d) Albert Peasemarch
   e) Mervyn Spink

4. The Gentleman's Personal Gentleman who is not gentleman
   but a thief, stealing socks and a book, is   a) Montague
   b) Brinkley   c) Bracely   d) Bingley   e) b or d

5. A butler whose surname is by ironic coincidence the first
   name of his employer's first husband is   a) Benson
   b) Spenser   c) Webster   d) Leicester   e) Worcester

6. A butler whose surname is also the surname of a Princess
   is   a) Mervo   b) Marvin   c) Dwornitzchek   d) Bannister
   e) Brabazon

7. Sir Roderick Glossop, for purposes of observing a
   prospective client, performs as a butler named
   a) Bluefish   b) Fisher   c) Swordfish   d) Haddock
   e) Minnow

8. Aunt Agatha's butler is   a) Spenser   b) Buncombe
   c) Litchfield   c) Purvis   d) a or c   e) none of the above

9. No butler in Wodehouse is named   a) Jeeves   b) Sturgis
   c) Keggs   d) Beach   e) Bulstrode

10. The butler who rides a motorcycle is   a) Spink
    b) Spenser   c) Sprockett   d) Swordfish   e) Spanner

11. Uncharacteristically young, slender and untrustworthy, is the
    pig-stealing butler   a) Bulstrode   b) Binstead
    c) Dalgleish   d) Beach   e) Bagshott.

12. Jeeves's Uncle Charlie is butler to   a) Spenser Gregson
    b) Aubrey Upjohn   c) Thomas Travers   d) Esmond
    Haddock   e) Myrtle Chuffnell

13. An eponymous butler is   a) Fogg   b) Robb   c) Noggs
    d) Steele   e) Bigger

14. Serves as butler to William Egerton Bamfylde Ossingham
    Belfry: a) Jeeves   b) Keggs   c) Beach   d) Bingley
    e) Seppings

15. The butler upon whose upper slopes ice formed is
    a) Bosher   b) Beach   c) Blizzard   d) Winters   e) Skidmore

16. A kind of Yuppy Butler who, in the Wodehouse canon, ends
    up with a butler of his own is   a) Beauregard
    b) Bosher   c) Bingley   d) Blizzard   e) no such thing.

17. A Butler to a former butler, unique in Wodehouse literature
    if not in life, is   a) Bronte   b) Bastable   c) Bronchitis
    d) Bulstrode   e) no such thing.

18. Aunt Dahlia's butler is   a) Steppings   b) Steptoe
    c) Stepins   d) Seppings   e) Shrimp.

19. A Butler whose namesake wrote a Pelican book is
    a) Barter   b) Binstead   c) Whipple   d) Wells   e) Whiteside.

20. A Butler who has more than usual to do with the furniture
    is   a) Chippendale   b) Chaffinch   c) Christie
    d) Sotheby   e) Soames.

21. Lord Ickenham's Butler is   a) Keggs   b) Coggs
    c) Sprockett   d) Bluffinghame   e) Moffinghame.

22. In the play version of *Leave It to Psmith* the Butler is
    a) Bellows b) Beddoes c) Stirrup d) Swizzle e) Beach.

23. A bottle-strewing Butler is a) Bosham b) Bloggs
    c) Phipps d) Framer e) Farmer.

24. The Butler who Did it is a) Craymore b) Crayfish
    c) Stanmore d) Keggs e) Coggs.

25. The Butler with a Bullfinch who, he fears, might know too
    much is a) Silversmith b) Chaffinch c) Beach
    d) Chibnall e) Barter.

26. The butler whose dog writes his own autobiographical tale
    is a) Webster b) Wells c) Weeks d) Ferris e) Maple.

27. The Butler Uncle Tom Travers traded for an oviform
    chocolate pot on three scroll feet is a) Ponsonby
    b) Pomegranate c) Pomeroy d) Ponders e) Seppings.

ANSWERS

CHAPTER XIV • THE BUTLER DID IT

1 — *e*

2 — *d*

3 — *d*

4 — *e*

5 — *b* (*Mrs. Spenser Gregson*)

6 — *c* (The Play's the Thing)

7 — *c*

8 — *d* (*"Jeeves and the Impending Doom,"* *"Sir Roderick Comes to Lunch"*)

9 — *a*

10 — *a*

11 — *b*

12 — *d*

13 — *b*

14 — *a*

15 — *b*

16 — *c* (Much Obliged, Jeeves)

17 — *b* (Much Obliged, Jeeves)

18 — *d*

19 — *b* (*Arthur W. Binstead*, A Pink 'Un and a Pelican)

20 — *a*

21 — *b*

22 — *a*

23 — *c* (The Old Reliable)

24 — *d*

25 — *c* (Pigs Have Wings, *et passim*)

26 — *c* (The Man with 2 Left Feet)

27 — *c* (The Code of the Woosters)

CHAPTER XV

PLUMS DE MA TANTE

I n each puzzle, all of the missing words are anagrams of each other: the missing words can all be completed using the same letters.

1.

At Blandings, famed for frauds and _ _ _ _ s,
The Empress stands alone:
Regarding all impostors _ _ _ _ ,
She surely holds her own.
From her we all might take a tip—
With bran _ _ _ _ take a little nip.

2.

From Malvern House to _ _ _ _ _' _ halls
The Bungler Wooster, as a boy,
Had yet to pack them in the stalls
By singing "Sonny Boy,"
And at the _ _ _ _ _ of his voice
Would many a Master turn to _ _ _ _ _ ,
Express in dismal _ _ _ _ _ his choice:
"Leave me. I would be alone."
No _ _ _ _ _ he, his voice would break:
"Alas, these _ _ _ _ _ I cannot take!"

3.

"He gazed at the girl like an _ _ _ _ _ _ _ goggling at a brass doorknob." (*Uncle Fred in the Springtime*)

Harsh words: Oofy Prosser is a _ _ _ _   _ _ _ _ .

Ukridge, almost invariably, avoids picking up bills _ _ _ _ _ _ _.

This fabulous bird of Araby, _ _ _ _   _ _ _ _ , is bigger than Aunt Dahlia's Emu, a Large Australian Bird made famous by crossword puzzles.

"_   _ _ _ _ _ _ _!" exclaimed the profane Vicar, spattering an Orphrey with ill-considered ink.

4.

Aloof, reserved, aesthetical,
Jeeves rarely goes out on dates,
Considering them heretical
And preferring _ _ _ _ _ to _ _ _ _ _ .
On _ _ _ _ _ he might woodenly opine,
On fish than _ _ _ _ _ he'd rather dine;
He does not _ _ _ _ _ _ and otherwise
_ _ _ _ _ little form of exercise;
But he'd _ _ _ _ _ _ a meal
On his Ideal:
To Quote From A through Yeats.

5.

The Wodehouse Tomboy's on the _ _ _ _
Wondering whether to wed or not;
It may be that what she'd like most
Is a highly paid executive _ _ _ _ ;
She may make money, that is clear,
If she _ _ _ _ _ for a career.
Nothing much will _ _ _ _ _ her then,
Especially if she dislikes men.
_ _ _ _ in her field, she then will shirk
What some men think is woman's work.
Such women and men, it's plain to see,
Very often disagree;
But they would *all* accept these words:
Washing _ _ _ _ is for the birds!

ANSWERS

1.

At Blandings, famed for frauds and S H A M S,
The Empress stands alone:
Regarding all impostors H A M S,
She surely holds her own.
From her we all might take a tip—
With bran M A S H takes a little nip.

2.

From Malvern House to E T O N 's halls
The Bungler Wooster, as a boy,
Had yet to pack them in the stalls
By singing "Sonny Boy,"
And at the O N S E T of his voice
Would many a Master turn to S T O N E,
Express in dismal T O N E S his choice:
"Leave me. I would be alone."
No S T E N O he, his voice would break:
"Alas, these N O T E S I cannot take!"

3.

"He gazed at the girl like an O S T R I C H goggling at a brass
doorknob." (Uncle Fred in the Springtime)

Harsh words: Oofy Prosser is a R I C H S O T.

Ukridge, almost invariably, avoids picking up bills O R C H I T S.

This fabulous bird of Araby, T H I S R O C, is bigger than Aunt
Dahlia's Emu, a Large Australian Bird made famous by crossword
puzzles.

"O C H R I S T!" exclaimed the profane Vicar, spattering an
Orphrey with ill-considered ink.

4.

Aloof, reserved, aesthetical,
Jeeves rarely goes out on dates,
Considering them heretical
And preferring K E A T S *to* K A T E S .
On T E A K S *he might woodenly opine,*
On fish than S T E A K *he'd rather dine;*
He does not S K A T E *and otherwise*
T A K E S *little form of exercise;*
But he'd S T A K E *a meal*
On his Ideal:
To Quote From A through Yeats.

5.

The Wodehouse Tomboy's on the S P O T
Wondering whether to wed or not;
It may be that what she'd like most
Is a highly paid executive P O S T ;
She may make money, that is clear,
If she O P T S *for a career.*
Nothing much will S T O P *her then,*
Especially if she dislikes men.
T O P S *in her field, she then will shirk*
What some men think is woman's work.
Such women and men, it's plain to see,
Very often disagree;
But they would all *accept these words:*
Washing P O T S *is for the birds!*

LE MENU

P lace each of the following menus, whether actually served or not, among the Wodehouse Chefs d'Oeuvre. Who did (or did not) eat it, and where?

1

Clear soup.
Halibut.
Chicken en casserole.
Savoury.

2

A few plovers' eggs.
A cup of soup.
A touch of cold salmon.
Cold curry.
Gosseberry tart and cream.
Cheese.

3

A dog biscuit.
A glass of water.

4

Cold consommé.
A cutlet.
Savoury.
Lemon-squash, iced.

5

Muffins.
Jam.
Ham.
Cake.
Scrambled eggs.
Sardines.
Tea.

6

Cold veal and ham pie.
Fruit cake.
A macaroon.
Cocoa.

7

Hors d'oeuvres variés.
Consommé Julienne.
Fried smelts.
Faisan Rôti.
Soufflé au Maître d'hôtel.
Scotch Woodcock.

8

Consommé Paté d'Italie.
Paupiettes de Sole a la Princesse.
Caneton d'Aylesbury a la Broche.
Les Fromages.
Les Fruits.
Le Café.

9

Barley meal.
Maize meal.
Linseed meal.
Potatoes.
Separated buttermilk.

10

Smoked salmon.
Mushroom soup.
Filet of sole.
Hungarian goulash.
  Mashed Potatoes.
  Buttered Beets.
  Buttered Beans.
Asparagus with mayonnaise.
Ambrosia Chiffon Pie.
Cheese.
Fruit.
Petits Fours.

11

Le Caviar Frais.
Le Consommé aux Pommes d'Amour.
Les Sylphides à la Crème d'Ecrevisses.
Les Fried Smelts.
Le Bird of Some Kind.
  with Chipped Potatoes.
Le Ice Cream.
Les Fruits.
Le Café.

12

Caviar.
Clear soup.
Roast chicken
  with Bread Sauce and
  two Veg.
Poires Hélĕne.
Jam Omelette.

13

Flesh.
Wine.
Roly-poly pudding,
    with lots of jam in it.
Oysters.
Ice cream.
Chocolates
    with that goo-ey, slithery stuff
    in the middle.

14
Curried Lobster

Two two-pound lobsters, two teaspoon-
fuls lemon juice, half teaspoonful
curry powder, two tablespoonfuls butter, one tablespoon flour, one cup
scalded milk, one cup cracker crumbs,
half teaspoonful salt, quarter teaspoonful pepper.
Cream the butter and flour and add
the scalded milk, then add the lemon
juice, curry powder, salt and pepper.
Remove the lobster meat from the shells
and cut into half-inch cubes. Add the
latter to the sauce. Refill the lobster
shells, cover with buttered crumbs, and
bake until the crumbs are brown.

15

Grade-A soup.
Toothsome fish.
Salmi of game which even Anatole might have been
    proud to sponsor.
Asparagus.
A jam omelette.
Some spirited sardines on toast.

16 [* * *]
Possibly a touch of smoked salmon
or a bit of melon.
A little clear soup.
Truite bleue and
The Wing of a Chicken.
Some sort of *soufflé*.

ANSWERS

CHAPTER XVI · LE MENU

1. The World of Jeeves, *Introduction. Proposed by PGW as suitable to accompany "Jeeves and the Old School-Friend."*

2. *"Bingo and the Little Woman." Bingo and Bertie at the Senior Liberal Club.*

3. *"Sir Roderick Comes to Lunch." Proposed by Bertie to Aunt Agatha, facetiously, as a menu which would about meet the case.*

4. *"Sir Roderick Comes to Lunch." What Jeeves actually gives Bertie and Sir Roderick.*

5. *"Comrade Bingo." The tea menu which Bingo requests for Comrade Butt and the Sons of the Red Dawn.*

6. *"Jeeves in the Springtime." What Bingo orders for lunch at the blighted tea and bun shop about fifty yards east of the Ritz where Mabel is waitress.*

7. **Louder and Funnier.** *As devoured by the publishers Faber (major) and Faber (minor) as an essential prerequisite for enjoying the book.*

8. **"Clustering Round Young Bingo"** *Served at the Little Residence, 39, Magnolia Road, London N.W. 8, to Mr. and Mrs. Thomas Portarlington Travers and Bertram Wilberforce Wooster, prepared by Anatole. This is the dinner which started all the trouble about Anatole, appearing here for the first time.*

9. *The daily menu of the Empress as prescribed by Whiffle, aiming at the old midseason form, and amounting to not less than 57,800 calories. See* **Pigs Have Wings,** *Chapter One, for this particular swell (and swelling) swill,. varied passim.*

10. **Pigs Have Wings.** *Sir Gregory Parsloe-Parsloe, jilted, takes to food at Matchingham Hall, Matchingham.*

11. **Jeeves and the Feudal Spirit.** *Served at Brinkley Court, Brinkley-cum-Snodsfield-in-the-Marsh, to: G. D'Arcy Cheesewright, Lady Florence Craye, Percival Gorringe, Mr. and Mrs. Thomas Portarlington Travers, Mr. and Mrs. Lemuel Gengulphus Trotter, and Bertram Wilberforce Wooster. Though prepared by Anatole, "for all the effect it had on the Wooster soul it might have been corned beef hash."*

12. **Something Fishy.** *The dinner not prepared by Jane Benedick for her Uncle George, Sixth Viscount Uffenham, at Castlewood, Mulberry Grove, Valley Fields, London SE 21, the home of Mr. Augustus Keggs.*

13. **"Episode of the Dog McIntosh."** *This is the revolting menu as bespoke by Bertie on behalf of Pop Blumenfeld and his foul son when they are to lunch at Bertie's flat.*

14. **Something Fresh.** *Ashe Marson at Blandings: bedtime reading for the dyspeptic, insomniac Mr. Peters. Serves six.*

15. *Dinner at Totleigh Towers, which turns to ashes in Bertie's m.* (**The Code of the Woosters,** *Chapter Six*)

16. *Archibald Mulliner yearns for, but can't swing. ("Archibald and the Masses")*

LE MOT JUSTE—
VOCABULARY QUIZ

D *efine each of the following:*

1. basilisk

2. beak

3. bootless

4. doo-dah

5. faugh

6. goop

7. gowans

8. mulct

9. nifty

10. odalisque

11. oofy

12. oojah-cum-spiff

13. pipterino

14. porpentine

15. prosser

16. rannygazoo

17. smeller

18. tchah

19. wambler

20. whangee

21. wonky

ANSWERS

CHAPTER XVII · LE MOT JUSTE

1. *basilisk: a legendary reptile. They have eyes like aunts: a glance is fatal. (Passim)*

2. *beak: a judge,* e.g. *Sir Watkyn Bassett. Also, a schoolmaster.* (Jeeves and the Feudal Spirit, *Chapter 6, and passim*)

3. *bootless: fruitless.* (Stiff Upper Lip, Jeeves, *passim.*)

4. *doo-dah: dither as in "All of a . . . ."* (The Code of the Woosters, *Chapter 5;* Jeeves and the Feudal Spirit, *Chapter 14*)

5. *faugh: an expression of regretful contempt. "The only time I've ever heard the word." ("The Ordeal of Young Tuppy") "Fore? Like at Golf?"* (Joy in the Morning, *Chapter 18*) *See also* The Code of the Woosters, *Chapter 2;* Jeeves in the Offing, *Chapter 7.*

6. *goop: a gaby; a chump.* (Joy in the Morning; *passim*)

7. *gowans: wild-flowers. Uncle Fred plucks them fine, passim.*

8. *mulct: to fine, or to win in a law-suit.* (The Code of the Woosters, *numerous uses passim, always followed by the phrase "for heavy damages."*)

9. *nifty: a bon mot, neat saying, or literary allusion.* (Heavy Weather, *Chapter 15: Pilbeam pinches Monty Bodkin's about the Den of the Secret Nine.*)

10. *odalisques: Not aunts, Sir.* (The Code of the Woosters)

11. *oofy: rich (slang)*

12. *oojah-cum-spiff: fine and dandy; hunkey-dory; A-OK.* Passim.

13. *pipterino: superlative of "pip" or "pippin." A very good-looking girl.* (Jeeves and the Feudal Spirit, *Chapter 17; passim.*)

14. *porpentine: porcupine. Shakespeare never did get it right.* (Passim, *and* Jeeves in the Offing, *Chapters 11 and 20;* Joy in the Morning, *Chapt. 20*)

15. *prosser: a putter-on of airs; a stuffed shirt. Oofy Prosser is an oofy prosser.*

16. *rannygazoo: monkey-business; chicanery. Passim.*

17. *smeller: a purler. A fall such as Constable Eustace Oates takes from his bicycle in* The Code of the Woosters.

18. *tchah: faugh.* (Joy in the Morning, *Chapter 18; passim*)

19. *wambler: one who wambles, pie-faced and wretchedly. In "The Spot of Art" Aunt Dahlia calls Bertie one.*

20. *whangee: a riding crop, or a walking stick, used to chase young Bertram caught smoking a good cigar. (Passim)*

21. *wonky: a bit thick. ("The Spot of Art")*

SCRAMBLED EGG

"One cannot make an omelette without breaking eggs."—One of Jeeves's gags.

*I*n each puzzle, unscrambling the individual rows will name people, places or things which are the topic of the puzzle. Then, the encircled letters can be arranged to complete the bottom line identifying that topic.

1

1. TRECHTUB   CERIP

2. DINEW   TPTO

3. CERPY   BIRPGRITH

4. ORGEEG   RILCY   BOLVEDELLEW

5. CAMINO   MOIMNSS

6. They are _ _ _ _   _ _ _ _ _ _ _ _ ' _   _ _ _ _
   _ _ _ _ _ _ .

2

7. HMSTIP

8. PURRET   AXERBT

9. DANSY   LALERDENC

10. RAVENLED   GIRBGS

11. Each is __ __ __ __ __ __ __ __ __ __ __ __ __
    __ __ __ __ __ __ __ __ __ __.

3

12. LENOCY   CHATH

13. CHILDUW

14. RORWAH

15. NEOT

16. VALMERN   OUSHE

17. KRYWN

18. TS PHASAS

19. GAMLADEN

20. TS   BEGSERTHUAL

21. Each is __ __ __ __ __ __ __ __ ,   __ __ __ __ __ __ __ , or
    __ __ __ __ __ __ __ .

4

22. R NEJOS

23. REPYC LEBMAIP

24. ARLEDG NATSURTREH LAVI

25. SHEA SMORAN

26. J B KEOH

27. All except one _ _ _ _ _ _ _ _ _ _ _ _ _ _ _ _ .

5

28. DACKHOAS   CHADHEAE   KISHOE   *(The Mating Season)*

29. SROPSERS   EPP   SLIPL   *(Brinkmanship of Galahad Threepwood)*

30. GGUSS   THOOSEIN   *(Full Moon)*

31. RAMPATUNO   AHMS   *(Quick Service)*

32. BYLSGINSS   REPSUB   UPSOS   *("The Spot of Art")*

33. LANDONSODS   ODG   OYJ   *(passim)*

34. RIPCES   MERDA   VAILSIT   *(If I Were You)*

35. SHOFLE   *("The Heel of Achilles")*

36. All are _ _ _ _ _ _   _ _ _   _ _ _ _ _ _ _
    _ _ _ _ _ _ _ _ .

ANSWERS

CHAPTER XVIII · SCRAMBLED EGG

"One cannot make an omelette without breaking eggs." —One of Jeeves's gags

In each puzzle, unscrambling the individual rows will name people, places or things which are the topic of the puzzle. Then, the encircled letters can be arranged to complete the bottom line identifying that topic.

1

1. *TRECHTUB CERIP*

2. *DINEW TPTO*

3. *CERPY BIRPGRITH*

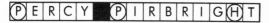

4. *ORGEEG RILCY BOLVEDELLEW*

5. *CAMINO MOIMNSS*

MONICA SIMMONS

6. *They are* ALL EMSWORTH'S PIG PEOPLE.

2

7. *HMSTIP*

P Ⓢ M I Ⓣ H

8. *PURRET   AXERBT*

Ⓡ U P Ⓔ R T   ▉ B Ⓐ X Ⓣ E R

9. *DANSY   LALERDENC*

S Ⓐ Ⓝ D Ⓨ   ▉ Ⓒ Ⓐ Ⓛ L Ⓔ N D E Ⓡ

10. *RAVENLED   GIRBGS*

Ⓛ Ⓐ V E Ⓝ Ⓓ E R   ▉ Ⓑ R Ⓘ Ⓖ G Ⓢ

11. *Each is* A S E C R E T A R Y A T
     B L A N D I N G S .

3

12. *LENOCY   CHATH*

C O L N E Y   H A T C H

13. *CHILDUW*

D U L W I C H

14. *RORWAH*

H A R R O W

15. *NEOT*

E T O N

16. *VALMERN   OUSHE*

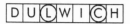

M A L V E R N   H O U S E

17. *KRYWN*

W R Y K N

18. *TS PHASAS*

S T   A S A P H S

19. *GAMLADEN*

M A G D A L E N

20. *TS   BEGSERTHUAL*

S T   E T H E L B U R G A S

21. *Each is* A   S C H O O L ,   C O L L E G E ,   *or*
   A S Y L U M .

4

22. *R NEJOS*

R ☐ J O N Ⓔ S

23. *REPYC LEBMAIP*

P E Ⓡ C Ⓨ ☐ Ⓟ Ⓘ Ⓛ B Ⓔ A M

24. *ARLEDG NATSURTREH LAVI*

G E R Ⓐ L D ☐ A N S Ⓣ R U T H Ⓔ R ☐ Ⓥ A Ⓘ L

25. *SHEA SMORAN*

A S H Ⓔ ☐ M A R Ⓢ O N

26. *J B KEOH*

J ☐ B ☐ H O Ⓚ E

27. *All except one* L I K E   P R I V A T E   E Y E S .

5

28. *DACKHOAS CHADHEAE KISHOE*   (The Mating Season)

| H | A | D | Ⓓ | O | C | K | S | ■ | H | E | A | Ⓓ | A | C | H | Ⓔ | ■ | H | O | K | I | E | S |

29. *SROPSERS EPP SLIPL*   (Brinkmanship of Galahad Threepwood)

| P | R | Ⓞ | S | S | E | R | S | ■ | P | Ⓔ | P | ■ | P | I | L | L | S |

30. *GGUSS THOOSEIN*   (Full Moon)

| S | U | G | G | S | ■ | Ⓢ | O | O | Ⓣ | H | I | N | E |

31. *RAMPATUNO AHMS*   (Quick Service)

| P | A | Ⓡ | A | Ⓜ | O | U | Ⓝ | T | ■ | H | A | M | S |

32. *BYLSGINSS REPSUB UPSOS*   (*"The Spot of Art"*)

| S | L | Ⓘ | N | G | S | B | Y | S | ■ | S | U | Ⓟ | E | R | B | ■ | S | O | U | P | Ⓢ |

33. *LANDONSODS ODG OYJ*   (*passim*)

| D | Ⓞ | N | A | L | D | S | O | N | S | ■ | D | O | G | ■ | J | Ⓞ | Y |

34. *RIPCES MERDA VAILSIT*   (If I Were You)

| P | Ⓡ | I | C | E | S | ■ | D | Ⓔ | R | M | Ⓐ | ■ | V | I | Ⓣ | A | L | I | S |

35. *SHOFLE*   (*"The Heel of Achilles"*)

| Ⓕ | L | Ⓔ | S | H | O |

36. *All are* F O O D S   O R   P A T E N T
R E M E D I E S .

BLANDINGS PARVA

R eading from left to right horizontally, diagonally upwards and downwards, and vertically from top to bottom, you can find in the box of letters below the names of 42 servants at Blandings Castle, tradespeople, constables, vicars and veterinarians and other residents of Market Blandings. All are Below Stairs, Behind the Green Baize Door, or Outside the Gates. Some are given their titles or additions, some not; some are given all their names, some first, last or last with first initial. Some will leap out at you; others will seek to retain the obscurity of their station. One further note for the class-conscious: if you think this is just a simple-minded or poor man's crossword puzzle, you'll soon think again. Do not disdain the clues, which appear in random order: without them, no one could solve this puzzle except Rupert Baxter and Richard Usborne.

```
M  A  R  L  E  N  E  W  E  L  L  B  E  L  O  V  E  D  W
M  C  A  L  L  I  S  T  E  R  B  U  L  S  T  R  O  D  E
E  R  I  G  G  S  P  O  O  L  E  A  M  O  R  G  A  N  P
R  P  S  E  L  T  H  A  M  G  C  H  A  R  L  E  S  R  R
R  P  O  T  T  O  E  N  V  I  B  A  N  K  S  P  L  E  I
I  R  L  E  W  K  S  W  N  C  O  O  P  E  R  I  K  O  C
D  I  D  E  H  E  G  O  V  E  N  S  O  U  S  R  E  P  E
E  C  E  L  M  S  M  U  R  P  H  Y  H  A  A  B  M  G  R
W  E  E  A  A  B  A  L  F  R  E  D  B  B  I  R  D  N  V
E  I  J  L  R  A  L  E  O  P  E  L  I  H  A  I  M  G  R
B  E  U  N  L  X  M  R  S  W  I  L  L  O  U  G  H  B  Y
B  V  D  I  E  T  L  L  I  V  O  U  L  E  S  H  E  W  T
E  O  S  D  N  E  E  H  M  O  U  S  Y  V  E  T  P  E  H
R  L  O  W  L  L  L  A  R  D  E  V  E  A  P  E  L  C  O
H  E  N  R  Y  Q  T  H  O  R  N  E  K  N  W  A  A  C  M
P  J  N  O  R  O  B  I  N  S  O  N· P  S  L  E  U  M  A
E  S  I  M  M  O  N  S  S  L  I  N  G  S  B  Y  B  A  S
I  R  S  F  O  S  B  E  R  R  Y  S  M  I  T  H  E  R  S
A  N  N  R  E  V  J  A  M  E  S  B  E  L  F  O  R  D  S
```

(Emily Elliot Gould suggested the puzzle. I made it up. Geoffrey Jaggard, David Jasen and Richard Usborne helped me to solve it.)

CLUES

1. Emsworth's Head Gardener before McAllister
2. Housekeeper at Blandings, name drawn from Dickens (*Our Mutual Friend*)
3. Under-butler to Beach
4. Footman at Blandings
5. First Footman at Blandings

6. Valet to Freddie Threepwood

7. Knife and Boots Boy at Blandings

8. Chauffeur at Blandings preceding Voules

9. The Prototype of Butlers

10. Footman at Blandings

11. Niffy Pigman

12. Blandings chauffeur after Slingsby

13. (First) Footman at Blandings

14. Emsworth's dour, hirsute Head Gardener

15. Emsworth's Second Gardener

16. Emsworth's retiring land agent, Pig-Girl namesake

17. Most men who have not been christened with this name acquire the name on becoming footmen, including Yours Truly, elsewise known as The Present Writer. At Blandings he *is* a Footman.

18. Another footman at Blandings

19. Emsworth's Pigman lacking mouth's roof

20. Lady Dora's Butler (Wiltshire House, Grosvenor Square)

21. Pig Girl

22. Cook at Blandings

23. Later Pigman at Blandings

24. Market Blandings Veterinarian

25. Chemist, High Street, Market Blandings

26. Landlord of the Emsworth Arms

27. Market Blandings Constable

28. Market Blandings Constable

29. Another Market Blandings Constable

30. Market Blandings Station Cab Proprietor

31. Vicar at Market Blandings

32. Market Blandings Physician

33. Barmaid at the Emsworth Arms

34. House Agent, High Street, Market Blandings

35. Lady Diana's Maid

36. Market Blandings Hairdresser/Barber

37. Empress's Veterinary Surgeon

38. Potboy at the Emsworth Arms (abbr.)

39. Lord Emsworth's Girlfriend's Brother

40. Hog-Calling Vicar's son

41. Neighboring rose-fancier

42. Blandings Library Cataloguer

ANSWERS

CHAPTER XIX • BLANDINGS PARVA

1. THORNE SF
2. MRS. TWEMLOW SF
3. MERRIDEW SF
4. JAMES SF
5. ALFRED Passim
6. JUDSON SF
7. BILLY SF
8. SLINGSBY SF
9. BEACH Passim
10. THOMAS Passim
11. PIRBRIGHT FP/HW
12. VOULES Passim
13. STOKES Passim
14. McALLISTER Passim
15. BARKER Custody
16. SIMMONS CWatb
17. CHARLES FM
18. HENRY UFISPR
19. POTT FM
20. RIGGS PW
21. MONICA PW
22. MRS. WILLOUGHBY PB

23. PRICE PB
24. WEBBER HW
25. BULSTRODE PW, BG
26. G. OVENS Passim
27. MURPHY SS
28. EVANS PH, PW, BG
29. MORGAN BG
30. JNO ROBINSON Passim
31. FOSBERRY HW
32. BIRD SN
33. MARLENE WELLBE-LOVED BG
34. COOPER PW
35. POOLE SB
36. BANKS LP
37. SMITHERS PH
38. ERB FM
39. ERN BC
40. JAMES BELFORD BC
41. WILLARD LP
42. EVE LP

A N S W E R   G R I D

Horizontal

```
M A R L E N E W E L L   B E L O V E D
M C A L L I S T E R   B U L S T R O D E
  R I G G S P O O L E     M O R G A N
              C H A R L E S
  P O T T         B A N K S
            C O O P E R
        G O V E N S
        M U R P H Y
        A L F R E D     B I R D

        M R S W I L L O U G H B Y
          V O U L E S

    W I L L A R D E V E
H E N R Y   T H O R N E
  J N O R O B I N S O N
  S I M M O N S S L I N G S B Y
    F O S B E R R Y S M I T H E R S
        J A M E S B E L F O R D
```

Vertical

M																		
E				S														
R				T														
R	P			O											P			
I	R			K											I			
D	I			E											R			
E	C			S											B			
W	E											B			R			
E		J										I			I			
B		U										L			G			
B		D										L	E		H			T
E		S										Y	V		T			H
R		O											A					O
		N											N					M
													S					A
																		S

Diagonal

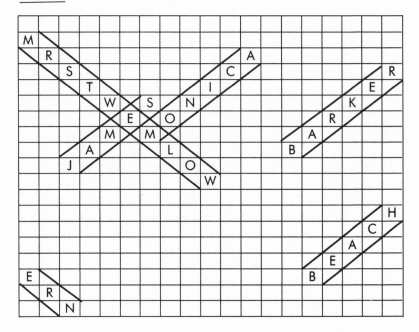

BLANK VERSES

F*illing in the missing names will enable you to answer the question which follows the verse.*

1

Her mother was a chorus girl, alone beloved of _ _ _ _ _ ;
   Pink satin and flesh-coloured tights he thought were very
     bonnie;
But, disapproving, his Papa sent him far away from

   _ _ _ _ _ .

   And that is why he now is glad to help her marry

   _ _ _ _ _ _ .

Who is she? (4) _____

2

A kindly and poetic cop,
   And one of New York's finest, he
Allows one simple 'phone call: Pop!
   Goes (5) _ _ _ _ _ _   _ _ _ _ _ _ _ _ 's dynasty.
Back at Blandings, take a look:
   Alas, Lady (6) _ _ _ _ _ _ _ _
(In her appearance like a cook)
   Feels duty-bound to spy on (7) _ _ _ _ ,
The dumbest blonde in Shropshire still
And governed by her mother's will.

Who is he? (8) _____

3

With many an old-time (9) _ _ _ _ _ _ _
  A notable carouser,
He now can't drink as (10) _ _ _ _ _ can.
  The scoundrel nobbled (11) _ _ _ _ _ _ .
Though limited, his belly can
  Still greet unnumbered dawns,
Digesting, still, as well he can,
  The story of the (12) _ _ _ _ _ _ .

Who is he? (13) _ _ _ _ _ _

4

"(14) _ _ _ _ _ _   _ _ _ _ _ _ _ _ _

  _ _ _ _ _ _ _ _ _
  "Known to his friends as (15) _ _ _ _ !
"No funnier writer has ever lived,
  "Nor will in the eons to come."
      —Peter Schwed

What dust wrapper flap bears this appropriate blurb? (16) _ _ _

5

"This is the trio of musical fame:
  "(17) _ _ _ _ _ _ and (18) _ _ _ _ _ _ _ _ _
    (19) _ _ _ _ ;
"Better than anyone else you can name,
  "(20) _ _ _ _ _ _ and (21) _ _ _ _ _ _ _ _ _
    (22) _ _ _ _ _ .
"Nobody knows what on earth they've been bitten by,
"All I can say is I mean to get lit an' buy
"Orchestra seats to the next one that's written by
  "(23) _ _ _ _ _ _ and (24) _ _ _ _ _ _ _ _ _
    (25) _ _ _ _ _ ."
      —Anonymous

Four shows written by this trio: (26) _ _ _ _ _ _
                (27) _ _ _ _ _ _
                (28) _ _ _ _ _ _
                (29) _ _ _ _ _ _

6
(A Limerick Sequence)

The destitute poor (30) _ _ _ _ _ _ _
   (31) _ _ _ _ _ _
Has practically given up hope:
  He could hardly be broker,
  His butler's a Joker,
And Constable (32) _ _ _ _ _ is a dope;

But he hasn't to worry for long.
Rich (33) _ _ _ _ _ _ is his for a song,
  Who, fulfilling his dream
  Pushes (34) _ _ _ _ _ in the stream
Where he'd dabbled his feet all along.

Now, the namesake of journalist (35) _ _ _ _
(Ernie Hemmingway's equal in style)
  As a guest at the Hall
  Doesn't matter at all,
But (36) _ _ _ _ would weep for his smile.

And amidst this spectacular fury
Is a (37) _ _ _ _ who is stuck on a jury;
(See Chapter II. Sorry for the interruption.)
  When *she's* broke she is merry—
  She'll now marry (38) _ _ _ _ _ —
He has got quite a lot of allure, he.

But . . . let's postpone the plot till tomorrow.
Its focus is on a (39) _ _ _ _ _ _ _ _ _ _ _ _ ,
  Who himself would attest
  "(40) _ . _ . _ _ _ _ _ _ _ _ _ is best,
"And was nothing if he was not thorough."

(41) What novel is all this about, then? _____

7

(A Sonnet Sequence)

Well past the hour of the setting sun,
  As we smoked pipes and nursed our pints of best
  Bitter, drawn here at the (42) _ _ _ _ _ _ ' _
    _ _ _ _ ,
My nephew (43) _ _ _ _ _ _ _ _ _ _ . . ." he had begun,
About a curate—young, extremely pale,
  Whose Aunt once sent him some embracing tonic.
  But going further here would be ironic,
For everyone amongst us knows the tale.
  The trouble with the tale of (44) _ _ _ _ - _ - _ _ _ _
    Is that it is incredible—e'en here,
      Where (45) _ _ _ _ _ _ _ _ has told gigantic lies,
    And anglers lie routinely in their beer.
  The oldest dog has known that since a pup. Oh,
    Trying tales are worse than tying flies!

When (46) _ _ _ _ _ _ _ _ _ _ begins a tale,
  The stoutest of us grabs his rod, and reels:
Though stout himself, he makes the stoutest quail,
  And I am here to tell you how it feels.
Though shooting squab is easy, though duck soup
  Is sitting pretty waiting for the bite
Of Fish, the (47) _ _ _ _ _ _ ' _ _ _ _ _ 's one loop-
  Hole is that (48) _ _ _ 's there every night!
No angler rests while that prodigious fish
  At large throughout our ken swims. No surprise,
One night then, when we granted our own wish,
  And stared, like (49) _ _ _ _ _ _ _ _ _ _ _ , with
    eagle eyes
    At him, then made our wish specific,
    And chased him half the way to the
    (50) _ _ _ _ _ _ _ !

(51) The Stella, Beatrice, Delia or Dark Lady of these sonnets is,
of course, the masculine _____ .

ANSWERS

Her mother was a chorus girl, alone beloved of G A L L Y*;*
  Pink satin and flesh-coloured tights he thought were very bonnie;
But, disapproving, his Papa sent him far away from D O L L Y*.*
  And that is why he now is glad to help her marry R O N N I E*.*

Who is she? (4) ___ SUE BROWN ___

2

A kindly and poetic cop,
  And one of New York's finest, he
Allows one simple 'phone call: Pop!
  Goes (5) T I P T O N   P L I M S O L L*'s dynasty.*
Back at Blandings, take a look:
  Alas, Lady (6) H E R M I O N E
(In her appearance like a cook)
  Feels duty-bound to spy on (7) V E E*,*
The dumbest blonde in Shropshire still
And governed by her mother's will.   .

Who is he? (8) ___ OFFICER GARROWAY ___

3

With many an old-time (9) P E L I C A N
  A notable carouser,
He now can't drink as (10) G A L L Y *can.*
  The scoundrel nobbled (11) T O W S E R*.*
Though limited, his belly can
  Still greet unnumbered dawns,
Digesting, still, as well he can,
  The story of the (12) P R A W N S*.*

Who is he? (13) ___ SIR GREGORY ("TUBBY") PARSLOE-PARLSOE, BART. ___

4

"*(14)* P E L H A M   G R E N V I L L E
     W O D E H O U S E
"*Known to his friends as* *(15)* P L U M*!*
"*No funnier writer has ever lived,*
  "*Nor will in the eons to come.*"
     —Peter Schwed

What dust wrapper flap bears this appropriate blurb? *(16)*   PLUM PIE

5

"*This is the trio of musical fame:*
  "*(17)* B O L T O N *and* *(18)* W O D E H O U S E
   (19) K E R N*;*
"*Better than anyone else you can name,*
  "*(20)* B O L T O N *and* *(21)* W O D E H O U S E
   (22) K E R N*.*
"*Nobody knows what on earth they've been bitten by,*
"*All I can say is I mean to get lit an' buy*
"*Orchestra seats to the next one that's written by*
  "*(23)* B O L T O N *and* *(24)* W O D E H O U S E
   (25) K E R N*."*
     —Anonymous

Four shows written by this trio: *(26)*   OH, BOY!
                                    (27)   SITTING PRETTY
                                    (28)   HAVE A HEART
                                    (29)   LEAVE IT TO JANE
                                              OH, LADY LADY!
                                              MISS 1917

6
(A Limerick Sequence)

The destitute poor (30) C R I S P I N *(31)* S C R O P E
Has practically given up hope:
  He could hardly be broker,
  His butler's a Joker,
And Constable (32) S I M M S *is a dope;*

But the hasn't to worry for long.
Rich (33) B A R N E Y *is his for a song,*
  Who, fulfilling his dream
  Pushes (34) S I M M S *in the stream*
Where he'd dabbled his feet all along.

Now, the namesake of journalist (35) P Y L E
(Ernie Hemmingway's equal in style)
  As a guest at the Hall
  Doesn't matter at all,
But (36) V E R A *would weep for his smile.*

And amidst this spectacular fury
Is a (37) J A N E *who is stuck on a jury;*
(See Chapter II. Sorry for the interruption.)
  When she's broke she is merry—
  She'll now marry (38) J E R R Y —
He has got quite a lot of allure, he.

But . . . let's postpone the plot till tomorrow.
Its focus is on a (39) G A I N S B O R O U G H,
  Who himself would attest
  "(40) P . G . W O D E H O U S E *is best,*
"And was nothing if he was not thorough."

(41) What novel is all this about, then?   THE GIRL IN BLUE

7

(A Sonnet Sequence)

Well past the hour of the setting sun,
 As we smoked pipes and nursed our pints of best
 Bitter, drawn here at the (42) A N G L E R'S R E S T,
My nephew (43) A U G U S T I N E . . ." *he had begun,*
About a curate—young, extremely pale,
 Whose Aunt once sent him some embracing tonic.
 But going further here would be ironic,
For everyone amongst us knows the tale.

 The trouble with the tale of (44) B U C K-U-U P P O
 Is that it is incredible—e'en here,
  Where (45) M U L L I N E R *has told gigantic lies,*
 And anglers lie routinely in their beer.
 The oldest dog has known that since a pup. Oh,
  Trying tales are worse than tying flies?

When (46) M R M U L L I N E R *begins a tale,*
 The stoutest of us grabs his rod, and reels:
Though stout himself, he makes the stoutest quail,
 And I am here to tell you how it feels.
Though shooting squab is easy, though duck soup
 Is sitting pretty waiting for the bite
Of Fish, the (47) A N G L E R'S R E S T's *one loop-*
 Hole is that (48) M R M's *there every night!*
No angler rests while that prodigious fish
 At large throughout our ken swims. No surprise,
One night then, when we granted our own wish,
 And stared, like (49) S T O U T C O R T E Z, *with eagle*
  eyes
 At him, then made our wish specific,
 And chased him half the way to the (50) P A C I F I C!

(51) The Stella, Beatrice, Delia or Dark Lady of these sonnets is,
of course, the masculine ___MR. MULLINER___ .

DUMB CHUMS

W odehouse was never happier than he was with a cat or two on his typewriter, another draped around his neck, a dachshund nibbling at the manuscript and another dachshund (call him Dachshund B) asking for more. Below, mate people with pets—Men with their Masters, as it were. Some answers (right column) may be used twice; some questions (left column) have two answers.

1. Buckingham Big Boy

2. an anonymous parrot

3. a bullfinch

4. Augustus

5. Pomona

6. Bottles

7. Cyril

8. 4 Pekes, 2 Poms, 5 Sea hams Etc.

9. Lysander

10. Empress of Blandings

11. Ambrose

12. Sam Goldwyn

13. McIntosh

a. Mrs. Spottsworth

b. Agatha Spenser Gregson

c. Sir Gregory Parsloe-Parsloe

d. Marcella Tyrrwhitt

e. Madeline Bassett

f. Dahlia Travers

g. Theodore, Bishop of Bongo-Bongo

h. Lady Widdrington

i. Sebastian Beach

j. Ickenham Hall

k. The Rev. Beefy Bingham

l. Aurelia Cammarleigh

14. Pride of Matchingham

15. Bartholomew

16. Mittens

17. Webster

18. William (Canary)

19. Percy (Cat)

20. Poppet

21. Mike

22. Muriel

23. Reginald (Peke)

24. Francis (Cat)

25. Percy (Dog)

26. Susan (Peke)

27. Wilfred (Alligator)

28. Mortal Error (Cat)

29. Sidney (Snake)

30. Sham-Poo

31. a stable cat

32. *Ranuculi*

33. Simla (Racehorse)

34. Potato Chip (Racehorse)

35. Buster

36. Minnie (Collie) (*)

37. Patricia (Peke)

38. Aida (Pomeranian)

39. James (Cat)

40. Eustace (Monkey)

m. P.G. Wodehouse

n. Valerie Twistleton

o. Corky Pirbright

p. Clarence, 9th Earl of Emsworth

q. Lady Georgiana Beazley-Beazley

r. Lord Brancaster

s. Lady Ann Warblington

t. Georgiana, Lady Alcester

u. Lord Tilbury

v. Stephanie Byng

w. Phyllis Mills

x. William Egerton Bamfylde Ossingham Belfry

y. Lottie Blossom

z. Roland Moresby Attwater

aa. Lady Pauline Weatherby

bb. Wilmot, Lord Pershore

cc. Vanessa Cook's father

dd. Beale, handyman

ee. Nesta Ford Pett

ff. Nelly Bryant

gg. Mrs. Bingham

hh. Marlene Hibbs

ii. Mr. Roddis

jj. Beatrice Chavender

kk. Colonel James Briscoe

41. Clarence (Snake)
42. bees
43. Benjy
44. hens and bees
45. Rastus and Tommy (Bull-dogs)
46. Bob (Mongrel)
47. Edwin (Persian Cat)
48. Rollo
49. Whiskers
50. Bill (Parrot)

ll. Kate Trent
mm. Myrtle Watling
nn. Elizabeth Boyd
oo. Phoebe Wisdom
pp. Molly McEachern
qq. Lady Vera Mace
rr. Millie Ukridge
ss. Potato Chip
tt. William Bannister Win-field
uu. Augustus Fink-Nottle

ANSWERS

1 — *u*

2 — *ii/r* (Right Ho, Jeeves)

3 — *i*

4 — *f*

5 — *a*

6 — *k*

7 — *n*

8 — *t*

9 — *l*

10 — *p*

11 — *f* (Right Ho, Jeeves)

12 — *o*

13 — *b*

14 — *c*

15 — *v*

16 — *j* (Uncle Dynamite)

17 — *g*

18 — *d*

19 — *h*

20 — *w*

21 — *x*

22 — *s*

23 — *d*

24 — *q*

25 — *e/gg* (The Mating Season, Bachelors Anonymous)

26 — *t*

27 — *y*

28 — *mm*

29 — *z*

30 — *qq*

31 — *ss* (Aunts Aren't Gentlemen)

32 — *uu*

33 — *kk* (Aunts Aren't Gentlemen)

34 — *cc* (Aunts Aren't Gentlemen)

35 — *oo* (The Girl in Blue)

36 — *m*

37 — *jj*

38 — *ee*

39 — *nn*

40 — *aa*

41 — *aa*

42 — *nn*

43 — *hh*

44 — *ll*

45 — *pp*

46 — *dd*

47 — *rr*

48 — *bb*

49 — *tt*

50 — *ff*

FOR OPENERS . .
CALL ME ISHMAEL

"It *was the best of times, it was the worst of times." "Fog." "You don't know about me without you have read a book by the name of* The Adventures of Tom Sawyer." *Melville could do it, Dickens could, probably, do it best, Mark Twain could do it; Wodehouse could do it, too—write the first sentence of a novel. Here are some. What is the novel of which each of the following is the first sentence? To complicate matters, you have to fill in some names.*

1

After the thing was all over, when peril had ceased to loom and happy endings had been distributed in heaping handfuls and we were driving home with our hats on the side of our heads, I confessed to (1) _ _ _ _ _ _ that there had been moments during the recent proceedings when (2) _ _ _ _ _ _ _ _ _ _ _ _ _ _, though no weakling, had come very near the despair.

(3) What novel? _____

2

Into the face of the young man who sat on the terrace of the Hotel Magnifique at (4) _ _ _ _ _ _ there had crept a look of furtive shame, the shifty, hangdog look which announces that an Englishman is about to talk French.

(5) What novel? _____

3

On a day in June, at the hour when (6) _ _ _ _ _ _ moves abroad in quest of lunch, a young man stood at the entrance of the Bandolero Restaurant, looking earnestly up
(7) _: a large young man, in excellent condition, with a pleasant, good-humored, brown, clean-cut face.

(8) What novel? _____

(9) What young man? _____

4

The main smoking room of the Strollers' Club had been filling for the last half-hour, and was now nearly full.

(10) What novel? _____

5

The train of events leading up to the publication of the novel
(11) _ _ _ _ _ _ _ _ _ _ _ _ _ _ , a volume which, priced at twelve shillings and sixpence, was destined to create considerably more that twelve and a half bobsworth of alarm and despondency in one quarter and another, was set in motion in the smoking room of the (12) _ _ _ _ _ _ _ _ _ _ in the early afternoon of a Friday in July.

(13) What novel? _____

6

In spite of the invigorating scent of coffee which greeted him as he opened the door, it was with drawn face and dull eye that the willowy young man with the butter-coloured hair and rather prominent Adam's apple entered the breakfast room of
(14) _ _ _ _ _ _ _ _ _ _ _ , the Tudor mansion in Sussex recently purchased by Mrs. (15) _ _ _ _ _ _ _ _ _ _ _ _ _ _ _ of Los Angeles.

(16) What novel? _____

7

" 'Morning, Jeeves," I said.

(17) What story? _____

8

If you search that portion of the state of New York known as
(18) __ __ __ __ __ __ __ __ __ __ with a sufficiently powerful
magnifying glass, you will find, tucked away on the shore of the
Great South Bay, the tiny village of
(19) __ __ __ __ __ __ __ __ __ __ __ .

(20) What novel? _____

9

Inasmuch as the scene of this story is that historic pile,
(21) __ __ __ __ __ __ __ __ __ __ __ __ __ __ , in the county of
Hampshire, England, it would be an agreeable task to open it
with a leisurely description of the place, followed by some notes
on the history of the Earls of
(22) __ __ __ __ __ __ __ __ __ __ __ __ who have owned it since
the fifteenth century.

(23) What novel? _____

10

Sunshine pierced the haze that enveloped (24) __ __ __ __ __ __ .

(25) What novel? _____

11

(26) __ __ __ __ __ __ placed the sizzling eggs and b. on the
breakfast table, and (27) __ __ __ __ __ __ __ __
(__ __ __ __ __ __) __ __ __ __ __ __ __ and I, licking the lips,
squared our elbows and got down to it.

(28) What novel? _____

12

The residence of Mr. (29) __ __ __ __ __ __ __ __ __ , the well-
known financier, on Riverside Drive is one of the leading
eyesores of that breezy and expensive boulevard.

(30) What novel? _____

13

Mr. (31) _ _ _ _ _ _ _ _ _ _ _ _ stood with his back
to the empty grate—for the time was summer—watching with a
jaundiced eye the removal of his breakfast things.

(32) What novel? _ _ _ _ _ _

14

"Where *have* I seen that face before?" said a voice.

(33) What novel? (*) _ _ _ _ _ _

15

The refined moon which served (34) _ _ _ _ _ _ _ _ _ _
_ _ _ _ _ _ and district was nearly at its full, and the
ancestral home of (35) _ _ _ _ _ _ _ _ _ , _ _ _ _ _ _
_ _ _ _ _ _ _ _ _ _ _ _ _ _ _ , had for some hours
now been flooded by its silver rays.

(36) What novel? _ _ _ _ _ _

16

At the open window of the great library of
(37) _ _ _ _ _ _ _ _ _ _ _ _ _ _ _ _ _ , drooping like a
wet sock, as was his habit when he had nothing to prop his spine
against, the (38) _ _ _ _ _ _ _ _ _ _ _ _ _ _ _ _ ,
drooping like a wet sock, as was his habit when he had nothing
to prop his spine against, the (38) _ _ _ _ _ _
_ _ _ _ _ _ _ _ _ , that amiable and boneheaded peer, stood
gazing out over his domain.

(40) What novel? _ _ _ _ _ _

17

Mrs. (41) _ _ _ _ _ _ _ _ _ _ _ _ _ _ _ _
dismissed the hireling who had brought her automobile around
from the garage and seated herself at the wheel.

(42) What novel? _ _ _ _ _ _

18

On an afternoon in May, at the hour when (43) __ __ __ __ __ __
pauses in its labours to refresh itself with a bite of lunch, there
was taking place in the coffee-room of the (44) __ __ __ __ __ __
__ __ __ __ in (45) __ __ __ __ __ Street that pleasantest of
functions, a reunion of old school friends.

(46) The host at the meal was _____

(47) What novel? _____

19

"(48) __ __ __ __ __ __ __ ," I said, "may I speak frankly?"

(49) What novel? _____

20

It was a morning in the middle of April, and the
(50) __ __ __ __ __ __ __ __ family were consequently breakfasting
in comparative silence.

(51) What novel? _____

21

(52) __ __ __ __ __ __ __ __ __ __ __ __ __ __ __ __ looked
around him with a frown, and gritted his teeth.

(53) What novel? (*) _____

22

With a sudden sharp snort which, violent though it was,
expressed only feebly the disgust and indignation seething
within him, (54) __ __ __ __ __ __ __ __ __ __ __ __ __ laid down
the current number of (55) __ __ __ __ __ __ __ __ __ __ __ __
and took up the desk-telephone.

(56) What novel? _____

23

The roof of the (57) _ _ _ _ _ _ _ _
_ _ _ _ _ _ _ _ _ _ _ _ _ _ _ _ _ , near
(58) _ _ _ _ _ _ _ _ _ _ _ _ _ _ _ _ _ _ _ ,
(59) _ _ _ _ _ _ _ _ . (You're right: grammatically, it's *not* a *sentence*!)

(60) What novel? _ _ _ _ _ _

24

(61) _ _ _ _ _ _ _ _ _ _ _ _ _ _ gazed coldly at the breakfast-table.

(62) What novel? _ _ _ _ _ _

25

Spring had come to (63) _ _ _ _ _ _ _ _ , the eight-fifteen train from (64) _ _ _ _ _ _ _ _ _ _ had come to the (65) _ _ _ _ _ _ _ _ _ _ _ _ terminus, and (66) _ .
_ _ _ _ _ _ _ _ _ _ _ _ _ that stout economic royalist, had come to his downtown office, all set to prise another wad of currency out of the common people.

(67) What novel? _ _ _ _ _ _

26

The dinner given by (68) _ . _ . _ _ _ _ _ _ _ at his (69) _ _ _ _ _ _ _ residence on the night of September the 10th, 1929, was attended by eleven guests, most of them fat and all, except (70) _ _ _ _ _ _ _ _ _ _ _ _ _ _ _ _ , millionaires.

(71) What novel? _ _ _ _ _ _

27

(72) _ _ . _ _ _ _ _ _ _ _ _ _ _ , the well-known solicitor, head of the firm of (73) _ _ _ _ _ _ _ _ _ _ _ ,
_ _ _ _ _ _ _ _ _ _ _ , _ _ _ _ _ _ _ _ _ _ _ , and so on, of (74) _ _ _ _ _ _ _ _ ' _ _ _ _ _ _ _ _ _ _ _ ,
leaned back in his chair and said that he hoped he had made everything clear.

(75) What novel? _ _ _ _ _ _

28

The Sergeant of Police who sat at his desk in the dingy little
(76) _ _ _ _ _ _ police station was calm, stolid and
ponderous, giving the impression of being constructed of some
form of suet.

(77) What novel? _ _ _ _ _ _ _ _

29

(78) _ _ _ _ _ _ _ _ _ _ _ _ _ _ _ _ _ —pronounced
(79) _ _ _ _ _ _ _ _ _ —the seat of (80) _ _ _ _ _ _ _ _
_ _ _ _ _ _ _ _ _ _ _ _ _ _ _ _ _ _ _ _ _ _ _ _ _ ,
ninth (81) _ _ _ _ _ _ _ _ _ _ _ _ _ _ _ _ _ _ _ _ , is one
of those stately homes of (82) _ _ _ _ _ _ _ _ _ which were a
lot statelier in the good old days before the moth got at them.

(83) What novel? _ _ _ _ _ _ _ _

30

The waiter, who had slipped out to make a quick telephone call,
came back into the coffee-room of the (84) _ _ _ _ _ _
_ _ _ _ _ _ _ _ _ _ _ _ wearing the starry-eyed look of a
man who has just learned that he has backed a long-priced
winner.

(85) What novel? _ _ _ _ _ _ _ _

31

Fork in hand and crouched over the stove in the kitchen of his
large and inconvenient house, (86) _ _ _ _ _ _ _ _ _ _ in
the county of (87) _ _ _ _ _ _ _ _ , (88) _ _ _ _ _ _
_ _ _ _ _ _ _ _ _ had begun to scramble eggs in a frying
pan.

(89) What novel? _ _ _ _ _ _ _ _

ANSWERS

"It was the best of times, it was the worst of times." "Fog." "You don't know about me without you have read a book by the name of The Adventures of Tom Sawyer." *Melville could do it, Dickens could, probably, do it best, Mark Twain could do it; Wodehouse could do it, too—write the first sentence of a novel. Here are some. What is the novel of which each of the following is the first sentence? To complicate matters, you have to fill in some names.*

1

After the thing was all over, when peril had ceased to loom and happy endings had been distributed in heaping handfuls and we were driving home with our hats on the side of our heads, I confessed to (1) J E E V E S *that there had been moments during the recent proceedings when (2)* B E R T R A M   W O O S T E R, *though no weakling, had come very near to despair.*

(3) What novel?   JOY IN THE MORNING

2

Into the face of the young man who sat on the terrace of the Hotel Magnifique at (4) C A N N E S *there had crept a look of furtive shame, the shifty, hangdog look which announces that an Englishman is about to talk French.*

(5) What novel?   THE LUCK OF THE BODKINS

3

On a day in June, at the hour when (6) L O N D O N *moves abroad in quest of lunch, a young man stood at the entrance of the Bandolero Restaurant, looking earnestly up*
(7) S H A F T E S B U R Y   A V E N U E: *a large young man, in excellent condition, with a pleasant, good-humored, brown, clean-cut face.*

(8) What novel?   UNEASY MONEY

(9) What Young Man?   William FitzWilliam Delamere Chalmers, Lord Dawlish

4

The main smoking room of the Strollers' Club had been filling for the last half-hour, and was now nearly full.

(10) What novel?   THE INTRUSION OF JIMMY

5

The train of events leading up to the publication of the novel
(11) C O C K T A I L   T I M E, *a volume which, priced at twelve shillings and sixpence, was destined to create considerably more than twelve and a half bobsworth of alarm and despondency in one quarter and another, was set in motion in the smoking room of the*
(12) D R O N E S   C L U B *in the early afternoon of a Friday in July.*

(13) What novel?   COCKTAIL TIME

6

In spite of the invigorating scent of coffee which greeted him as he opened the door, it was with drawn face and dull eye that the willowy young man with the butter-coloured hair and rather prominent Adam's apple entered the breakfast room of (14) C L A I N E S   H A L L, *the Tudor mansion in Sussex recently purchased by Mrs. (15)* H O W A R D S T E P T O E *of Los Angeles.*

(16) What novel?   QUICK SERVICE

7

" 'Morning, Jeeves,'' I said.

(17) What story?   "JEEVES EXERTS THE OLD CEREBELLUM"

8

If you search that portion of the state of New York known as (18) L O N G   I S L A N D *with a sufficiently powerful magnifying glass, you will find, tucked away on the shore of the Great South Bay, the tiny village of (19)* B E N S O N B U R G.

(20) What novel?   FRENCH LEAVE

9

Inasmuch as the scene of this story is that historic pile, (21) B E L P H E R   C A S T L E, *in the country of Hampshire, England, it would be an agreeable task to open it with a leisurely description of the place, followed by some notes on the history of the Earls of (22)* M A R S H M O R E T O N *who have owned it since the fifteenth century.*

(23) What novel?   A DAMSEL IN DISTRESS

10

Sunshine pierced the haze that enveloped (24) L O N D O N.

(25) What novel?   HEAVY WEATHER

11

(26) J E E V E S *placed the sizzling eggs and b. on the breakfast table, and (27)* R E G I N A L D   (K I P P E R) H E R R I N G *and I, licking the lips, squared our elbows and got down to it.*

(28) What novel?   HOW RIGHT YOU ARE, JEEVES

12

The residence of Mr. (29) P E T E R   P E T T, *the well-known financier, on Riverside Drive is one of the leading eyesores of that breezy and expensive boulevard.*

(30) What novel?   PICCADILLY JIM

13

Mr. *(31)* J E R E M Y G A R N E T *stood with his back to the empty grate—for the time was summer—watching with a jaundiced eye the removal of his breakfast things.*

(32) What novel?   LOVE AMONG THE CHICKENS

14

"Where have *I seen that face before?" said a voice.*

(33) What novel? (*)   THE POTHUNTERS

15

The refined moon which served (34) B L A N D I N G S C A S T L E *and district was nearly as its full, and the ancestral home of (35)* C L A R E N C E , N I N T H E A R L O F E M S W O R T H , *had for some hours now been flooded by its silver rays.*

(36) What novel?   FULL MOON

16

At the open window of the great library of (37) B L A N D I N G S C A S T L E , *drooping like a wet sock, as was his habit when he had nothing to prop his spine against, the (38)* E A R L O F E M S W O R T H , *that amiable and boneheaded peer, stood gazing out over his domain.*

(40) What novel?   LEAVE IT TO PSMITH

17

Mrs. (41) L O R A D E L A N E P O R T E R *dismissed the hireling who had brought her automobile around from the garage and seated herself at the wheel.*

(42) What novel?   THE COMING OF BILL

18

On an afternoon in May, at the hour when (43) L O N D O N
*pauses in its labours to refresh itself with a bite of lunch, there was taking
place in the coffee-room of the (44)* D R O N E S   C L U B *in
(45)* D O V E R *Street that pleasantest of functions, a reunion of old
school friends.*

(46) The host at the meal was ___GODFREY EDWARD WINSTANELY BRENT,
LORD BISKERTON (BISCUIT)___ .

(47) What novel? ___BIG MONEY___ .

19

"(48) J E E V E S *," I said, "may I speak frankly?"*

(49) What novel? ___RIGHT HO, JEEVES / BRINKLEY MANOR___

20

*It was a morning in the middle of April, and the
(50)* J A C K S O N *family were consequently breakfasting in
comparative silence.*

(51) What novel? ___MIKE___

21

(52) C L A R E N C E   C H U G W A T E R *looked around
him with a frown, and gritted his teeth.*

(53) What novel? (*) ___THE SWOOP___

22

*With a sudden sharp snort which, violent though it was, expressed only
feebly the disgust and indignation seething within him, (54)* S I R
G E O R G E   P Y K E *laid down the current number of
(55)* S O C I E T Y   S P I C E *and took up the desk-telephone.*

(56) What novel? ___BILL THE CONQUEROR___

23

The roof of the (57) S H E R I D A N   A P A R T M E N T
H O U S E, *near (58)* W A S H I N G T O N
S Q U A R E, *(59)* N E W   Y O R K. *(You're right:
grammatically, it's* not a sentence!*)*

(60) What novel?   THE SMALL BACHELOR

24

(61) F R E D D I E   R O O K E *gazed coldly at the breakfast-
table.*

(62)   THE LITTLE WARRIOR   *What novel?*

25

Spring had come to (63) N E W   Y O R K, *the eight-fifteen train
from (64)* G R E A T   N E C K *had come to the (65)*
P E N N S Y L V A N I A *terminus, and (66)* G.
E L L E R Y   C O B B O L D *that stout economic royalist, had
come to his downtown office, all set to prise another wad of currency out of
the common people.*

(67) What novel?   SPRING FEVER

26

The dinner given by (68) J.J.   B U N Y A N *at his
(69)* N E W   Y O R K *residence on the night of September the 10th,
1929, was attended by eleven guests, most of them fat and all, except
(70)* M O R T I M E R   B A Y L I S S, *millionaires.*

(71) What novel?   SOMETHING FISHY/THE BUTLER DID IT

27

(72) M R.   S H O E S M I T H, *the well-known solicitor, head
of the firm of (73)* S H O E S M I T H,
S H O E S M I T H,   S H O E S M I T H, *and so on, of
(74)* L I N C O L N'S   I N N   F I E L D S, *leaned back in
his chair and said that he hoped he had made everything clear.*

(75) What novel?   MONEY IN THE BANK

28

The Sergeant of Police who sat at his desk in the dingy little
(76) P A R I S *police station was calm, stolid and ponderous, giving*
the impression of being constructed of some form of suet.

(77) What novel? BIFFIN'S MILLIONS/FROZEN ASSETS

29

(78) T O W C E S T E R
A B B E Y —*pronounced (79)* T O A S T E R
—*the seat of (80)* W I L L I A M
E G E R T O N O S S I N G H A M
B E L F R Y, *ninth (81)* E A R L O F
T O W C E S T E R, *is one of those stately homes of*
(82) ENGLAND *which were a lot statelier in the good old days*
before the moth got at them.

(83) What novel? THE RETURN OF JEEVES

30

The waiter, who had slipped out to make a quick telephone call, came back
into the coffee-room of the (84) G O O S E A N D
G H E R K I N *wearing the starry-eyed look of a man who had just*
learned that he had backed a long-priced winner.

(85) What novel? RING FOR JEEVES

31

Fork in hand and crouched over the stove in the kitchen of his large and
inconvenient house, (86) A S H B Y H A L L *in the county of*
(87) S U S S E X, *(88)* H E N R Y
P A R A D E N E *had begun to scramble eggs in a frying pan.*

(89) What novel? COMPANY FOR HENRY/THE PURLOINED PAPERWEIGHT

MULLINER KNIGHTS

M *atch each Mulliner with His (or, perhaps, Her) Métier.*

1. Adrian
2. Lancelot
3. Cyril
4. Augustine
5. Eustace
6. George
7. Wilfred
8. Osbert
9. Charlotte
10. Montrose
11. Bulstrode
12. Sacheverell
13. Alfred
14. Clarence
15. Reginald
16. Mordred
17. Brancepeth

a. Swiss Ambassador
b. Jade Collector
c. Assistant Director
d. Gaining Agricultural Confidence
e. Fiery Poet
f. Assistant Editor
g. "Old Man River"
h. Interior Decorator
i. Detective
j. Hollywood Writer
k. Non-smoking Portrait-Painting Ukelelist
l. Artist
m. Artist who Painted the Moustache Joyeuse
n. Crossword Puzzles
o. Poet

18. Ignatius   p. Novelist

19. (Cousin) Lady Wickham   q. Cosmetics

20. Egbert   r. Conjuror

                         s. Vicar

                         t. Photographer

ANSWERS

CHAPTER XXIII · MULLINER NIGHTS

1. *I*   11. *j*

2. *l*   12. *d*

3. *h*   13. *r*

4. *s*   14. *t*

5. *a*   15. *g*

6. *n*   16. *e*

7. *q*   17. *m*

8. *b*   18. *k*

9. *o*   19. *p*

10. *c*   20. *f*

CHAPTER XXIV

LE DERNIER CRI

F ill in the blanks to read *The Last Word* on seven distinct areas of
Wodehouse study: his own life, School, Golf, Ukridge, Mr. Mulliner,
*Blandings Castle, and Jeeves and Bertie. A full and correct paper will
receive the Publisher's Wodehouse Summa Cum Laude diploma. Kindly
submit your answers to Peter Herbert, editor of "Arcana Suprema," c/o
James H. Heineman, 475 Park Ave., New York, NY 10022.*

1

A sort of (1) _ _ _ _ _, (2) _ _ _ _ _ _, (3)
_ _ _ _ _ _, (4) _ _ _ _ _ _ _,
(5) _ _ _ _ _ _ _ _ _ _ sound, like a thousand eager
men drinking soup in a foreign restaurant. And, as he heard it,
Lord Emsworth uttered a cry of rapture.
The (6) _ _ _ _ _ _ _ was (7) _ _ _ _ _ _ _.

What's the story? (8) _____.

2

"Thank you, sir. I gave it to the (9) _ _ _ _ _ -
_ _ _ _ _ _ _ _ last night. A little more tea, sir?"

What's the story? (10) _____

What's "it"? _____

3

What it was that gave me that impression I do not know—
probably vision of the (11) _ _ _, _ _ _ _ _ _,
_ _ _ _ _ _ _ _   _ _ _ _ _ _ _ _.

What's the story? (12) _____

4

Letter received. Send immediately, C.O.D. three cases of the
(13) "_." "Blessed shall be thy (14) _ _ _ _ _ _ and thy
(15) _ _ _ _ _ _." Deuteronomy xxviii.5.
(16) _ _ _ _ _ _ _ _ _ _.

(17) What's the story? _____

5

He folded her in his arms, using the
(18) _ _ _ _ _ _ _ _ _ _ _ _ _ _   _ _ _ _.

What's the story? (19) _____

6

(20) _ _ _ _ _ said it distinctly reminded him of a thing
which had happened to a friend of a chap his brother had known
at (21) _ _ _ _ _ _ _ _ _ _.

(22) What is the novel? _____

(23) Who is the title character? _____

7

What did P.G. Wodehouse do until age 5?
(24) _ _ _ _   _ _ _ _ _ _

And where is that fact recorded?

(25) _____.

BIBLIOGRAPHY

In devising some of the questions and in documenting many of the answers, I have consulted the following works.

Connolly, Joseph. *P.G. Wodehouse: An Illustrated Biography.* London: Orbis, 1979.

Garrison, Daniel H. *Daniel Garrison's Who's Who in Wodehouse.* New York, Bern: Peter Lang, 1987.

Heineman, James H. and Bensen, Donald R., Editors. *P.G. Wodehouse/A Centenary Celebration / 1881-1981,* with A Bibliography by Eileen McIlvaine. New York, London: The Pierpont Morgan Library/Oxford University Press, 1981.

Jaggard, Geoffrey. *Blandings the Blest.* London: Macdonald & Co. Ltd., 1968.

Jaggard, Geoffrey. *Wooster's World.* London: Macdonald & Co. Ltd., 1967.

Jasen, David A. *A Bibliography and Reader's Guide to the First Editions of P.G. Wodehouse 2nd Edition.* London: Greenhill Books, Lionel Leventhal Limited, 1986.

Rosenthal, Harold and Warrack, John. *Concise Oxford Dictionary of Opera.* London: Oxford University Press, 1964.

Usborne, Richard. *A Wodehouse Companion.* London: Elm Tree, 1981.

Usborne, Richard. *Wodehouse at Work to the End.* London: Barrie & Jenkins, 1976.

PUBLICATIONS AND BOOKS PUBLISHED BY

H

JAMES H. HEINEMAN, INC.

FORMING A SERIES ON, AROUND AND BY
P.G. WODEHOUSE

SIR PELHAM WODEHOUSE OLD BOY   (1978)
by Richard Usborne
   (some signed)

P.G. WODEHOUSE 1881-1981   (1982)
by Frances Donaldson and Richard Usborne
   (some numbered)

THE TOAD AT HARROW   (1982)
by Charles E. Gould, Jr.
   (some signed and numbered)

THE GREAT SERMON HANDICAP   (1983)
by P.G. Wodehouse
   (some numbered)

THREE TALKS AND A FEW WORDS AT A FESTIVE   (1983)
OCCASION IN 1982
*by Richard Usborne, William Douglas-Home, Malcolm
Muggeridge and Angus Macintyre*

NUGGETS   (1983)
by P.G. Wodehouse, selected by Richard Usborne

THE GREAT SERMON HANDICAP   (1989)
by P.G. Wodehouse
   Rendered in English, Phonetic English, Latin,
French, Spanish, Italian, Portuguese, Rumanian,
Catalan and Rhaeto-Romansch

WHAT'S IN WODEHOUSE (1990)
OR JEEVES HAS GONE A-SHRIMPING AND THE
FAT PIG HAS GROWN EVEN STOUTER
by Charles E. Gould, Jr.

P.G. WODEHOUSE: A COMPREHENSIVE (1990)
BIBLIOGRAPHY AND CHECKLIST
*edited by Eileen McIlvaine and co-published with St. Paul's
Bibliographies.*

In preparation:

BOLTON, WODEHOUSE AND KERN
by Lee A. Davis

H

This book was designed by Beth Tondreau Design.
It was set in Spartan Light and Baskerville, and was printed
by
Port City Press, Inc. on Glatfelter paper and bound by
Port City Press, Inc.

H